1982

1983

1984

Labels to be released

MOUTON ROTHSCHILD *Paintings for the Labels, 1945~1981*

FOR PAULINE

MOUTON ROTHSCHILD

Paintings for the Labels, 1945~1981

A New York Graphic Society Book · Little, Brown and Company · Boston

This book was published to coincide with the European opening of the exhibition, *Mouton Rothschild: Paintings for the Labels 1945–1981*, at the Royal Scottish Academy, as part of the 1983 Edinburgh Festival.

Circulation of the exhibition in the United States of America is organized by the Smithsonian Institution Traveling Exhibition Service.

New York Graphic Society books are published by Little, Brown and Company. Published simultaneously in Canada by Little, Brown and Company (Canada) Limited.

First edition

Printed in Italy by Mondadori, Verona

Acknowledgments
We would like to thank the following for their valuable collaboration: Martine Courtiade, Christiane Giroud, Monique Jaget, Michel Bardin, Eusèbe Betès, Raoul Blondin, Michael Broadbent, Jean Dit Cazaux, Charles Flipo, Milton Greenstein, Jean Marais, André Pacitti, David Russell, Jacques Tajan.

The Catalogue
Written by Philippine de Rothschild
and Jean-Pierre de Beaumarchais
Translated by John Wells
Designed by Susan Marsh

The Exhibition
Designed by Francis Lacloche
Organized by Xavier de Eizaguirre

Photographs
Paul Almazy; H. J. Anders; Michel André; Atelier 53; Cecil Beaton; Pierre Berdoy; Brassaï; Maurice Chuzeville; Keith Collie; Martine Franck; Michel Geney; David Gould; Martin Holger; ITAC; Dimitri Kasterine; Jacques Monget; Norman Parkinson; Georges Routhier; Christian Vioujard

Material on pages 119–123 is from Michael Broadbent's *Great Vintage Wine Book*, © 1980 Mitchell Beazley Publishers Limited, Text © Michael Broadbent, and is reproduced with the kind permission of the publishers and the author. *The Great Vintage Wine Book* is published in the USA by Alfred Knopf, New York.

Library of Congress Cataloging in Publication Data
Rothschild, Philippine de.
   Mouton Rothschild: paintings for the labels, 1945–1981.
   "New York Graphic Society book."
   1. Wine labels.   2. Commercial art—History—20th century.   3. Mouton-Rothschild (Firm)   I. Title.
NC1002.L3R67   1983   759.06   83–9421
ISBN 0-8212-1555-8

Contents

Baron Philippe and Rajah

pour Philippine

Le vin

Il naît
Puis il vit
Mais point ne meurt
En l'homme il survit

C'est ouvrage divin
La nature en symbiose
Celle de l'âme humaine
A sa source assimilée

Reflet de ses créateurs
D'espoir grâce en l'attente
Le vin s'en va vêtu d'un verre
Porteur magique d'un message

L'art de grands maîtres
Apporte à nos étiquettes
Echos de l'âme de Mouton
L'image d'une ferveur

Tant vont les ans
Telle se crée
L'oeuvre
La vie
Le vin   Papa — (Baron Philippe)

(translation on page 132)

A Word of Introduction

Mouton Rothschild: hardly more than a speck on the map of France, four hundred miles southwest of Paris, in the middle of the Médoc; a few acres of vines along the Gironde, on the Atlantic coast north of Bordeaux. But Mouton Rothschild is also a name famous all over the world, a name that brings thousands of pilgrims every year to visit the birthplace of a wine treated with reverence in every corner of the globe.

It is an amazing success story, made possible only by the conjunction of soil, skill, a quirk of history, and the will of man — or rather, the will of one man in particular, Baron Philippe de Rothschild.

First the soil: Gently sloping ground littered with pebbles that hold the heat of the sun till after dusk, lying beside a river that waters the soil far beneath the surface. A climate of extremes, rainy winters, summers of heavy heat, storms driving in from the Atlantic. Gnarled and twisted, laboring to lay roots wider and deeper into the earth, the vine forges its individual character, to grow and mature in the wine through the dark years in the cellar. The soil itself as unpredictable as the turn of dice: from vines less than fifty feet apart come one wine that is merely very good and another that is unequaled anywhere on earth.

But even at Mouton, Nature cannot manage on her own; she needs a helping hand — the skill: selecting exactly the right type of vine, protecting it against its natural enemies, pruning and cherishing it until it comes to full maturity. Autumn, and the harvest: then comes the *égrappage* — the work of separating the grapes from the stem — and the fermentation in the vats, watched over and controlled by the *maîtres de chai*. The grape is transmuted into a great wine: Château Mouton Rothschild.

The quirk of history: A member of the Rothschild family bought the estate of Brane-Mouton in the mid-nineteenth century, immediately renaming it Mouton Rothschild. So two names were linked, a wine of the Médoc and a dynasty of highly civilized men who had taken Europe by storm, pioneers of railway building and international banking, who knew that improved communications would lead to greater conviviality. Whenever a great wine was poured, new friends would be made, opening up a new world of travel and adventure.

Finally the man: in 1922, Philippe de Rothschild, then only twenty, took over the management of Mouton at a time when it was badly in need of love and attention. Convinced that building on tradition was a sound investment in the future, he chose men who knew their jobs and set to work. As a result of his efforts, the estate was transformed. New methods and new ideas were introduced; at least one of them — the château bottling of the entire crop — was to have a profound influence on the whole wine trade of Bordeaux. And a long-sought goal was finally achieved: in 1973, Château Mouton Rothschild won the ultimate distinction of being numbered among the *Premiers Crus*.

A poet, a man of the theater and a lifelong friend of many great figures in the arts, Baron Philippe has always been conscious of the relationship between wine and the creative imagination. He has made it his mission to celebrate the connection and bring it more vividly to the attention of the public. With his wife Pauline, he has been tireless in seeking out works of art that would illuminate that single great theme in painting, sculpture, tapestries, and porcelain. The treasures they found were brought together at Mouton to form a unique collection in what was to become the Mouton Museum, housed in a former *chai* between the vats and the barrels of maturing wine.

It remained to transform the bottle itself into a work of art by adding a decorative element to the old label. The first step was made in commissioning the great poster designer Carlu, who created the famous Cubist composition for the label of 1924. The idea was then abandoned and forgotten for twenty years, only to rise like a phoenix from the flames of war in 1945 in honor of the Allied victory, and, after that, simply in honor of Mouton Rothschild.

Ever since, enriched by the imaginations of great living artists, the labels have traveled the world, bearing witness to the marriage of wine and creativity celebrated in works of art from the wall paintings of Pompeii to Picasso's *Bacchanales*.

It is our privilege here to present the original works of all those artists who have contributed to make this collection unique. In these labels the creative imagination pays an annual tribute to wine for all the imaginative riches that wine, from the earliest-known religious cults and most ancient civilizations, has revealed to man.

Silver-gilt ram from Nuremberg (seventeenth century) on a bottle rack

Part One

THE COLLECTION

· ·

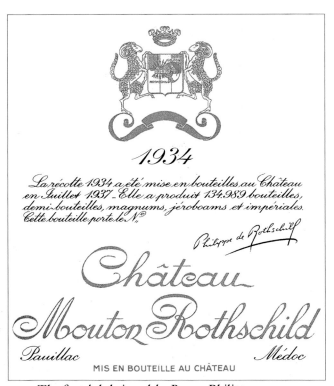

1859: The earliest Mouton Rothschild label in existence, printed six years after the purchase of Mouton by Baron Nathaniel de Rothschild

1929: The label in the late twenties

1934: The first label signed by Baron Philippe

1938: Unsigned label for Mouton Rothschild 1938. Bottled three years later in the absence of the owner, who was detained in a Vichy prison

The Story of the Labels

Until 1924, whatever its destination, the wine left the Mouton Rothschild estate in barrels — as it did on all estates in Bordeaux. The wine merchants, who bought a large proportion of the vintage, saw to everything else: they stored the wine while it was maturing in the casks, bottled it, labeled it, and sold it. With no direct control over the final product, the grower took little interest in the appearance of the label. The design, such as it was, was left entirely to the wine merchant.

In 1924 Mouton Rothschild instituted a revolutionary new practice: the entire vintage was bottled at the château; this was the first instance of the famous *mise en bouteilles au château*, and the procedure was soon adopted by the *Premiers Crus*. Château bottling inevitably had far-reaching consequences; the grower was now personally responsible to the consumer for the quality of the product. Consequently the labels took on a new function: they became the birth certificate, the official guarantee, the distinctive uniform of each individual bottle.

To draw attention to this new departure, Baron Philippe commissioned poster designer Jean Carlu to create an original label for the year 1924. His design remains one of the most successful examples of the influence of Cubism in commercial art, earning a place in this exhibition, though not in the present series. The same basic design was used again in 1925 and 1926.

Between 1928 and 1934, the Mouton Rothschild label underwent a number of adjustments.

In 1929 the device of the "Rams Rampant," still in use today, appeared. It is partly a pun on the word *mouton* — a sheep — and partly an allusion to Baron Philippe's birth sign, Aries, the Ram.

In 1934, an official declaration was added to the label specifying the total number of bottles produced that year: half bottles (*demi-bordelaises*), bottles (*bordelaises*), magnums, double magnums, jeroboams, and imperials.

That same year, the grower's signature also appeared on the label for the first time. This format remained unchanged until 1944, with four notable exceptions: the labels for 1938, 1939, 1940, and 1941 remained unsigned. Wine is bottled three years after the harvest, and these years would therefore have had to be signed between 1941 and 1944, when Baron Philippe was either in a Vichy jail or serving with the Free French Forces abroad.

Baron Philippe signing bottles of Mouton Rothschild 1977

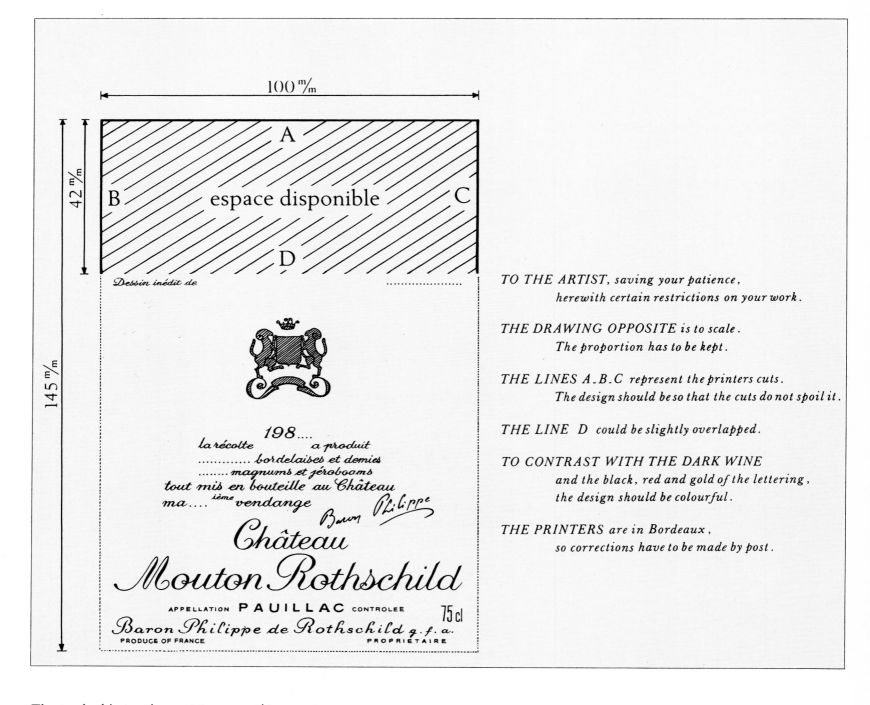

100 m/m

42 m/m

145 m/m

A

B   espace disponible   C

D

Dessin inédit de ....

198....
la récolte   a produit
.... *bordelaises et demies*
.... *magnums et jéroboams*
tout mis en bouteille au Château
ma.... ième *vendange*   Baron Philippe

Château
Mouton Rothschild

APPELLATION **PAUILLAC** CONTROLEE   75 cl

Baron Philippe de Rothschild g.f.a.
PRODUCE OF FRANCE   PROPRIÉTAIRE

TO THE ARTIST, saving your patience,
   herewith certain restrictions on your work.

THE DRAWING OPPOSITE is to scale.
   The proportion has to be kept.

THE LINES A.B.C represent the printers cuts.
   The design should be so that the cuts do not spoil it.

THE LINE D could be slightly overlapped.

TO CONTRAST WITH THE DARK WINE
   and the black, red and gold of the lettering,
   the design should be colourful.

THE PRINTERS are in Bordeaux,
   so corrections have to be made by post.

The standard instructions sent to every artist

THE PRESENT LABEL

At the end of the Second World War, Baron Philippe, home again and with the house free of German occupation, conceived the idea of dedicating the Mouton Rothschild vintage to Victory Year — *l'Année de la Victoire* — with an illustrated panel on the label.

What had been a "once-off" idea was to become a tradition: from 1946 onwards an important contemporary artist would be commissioned to illustrate the label with an original work. The Mouton Rothschild label had finally found its definitive form.

From the top:
· The reproduction of the work of art
· The Ram emblem
· The declaration of the number of bottles produced
· The proprietor's signature
· The name of the wine, Château Mouton Rothschild
· The year: from 1945 to 1958, it appears beneath the Ram emblem; from 1959 to 1973, it flanks the Ram emblem; and from 1974 onwards it returns to its original position.

There were to be two years in which no painting was commissioned: in 1953 the label celebrated the centenary of the purchase of the Mouton estate by Baron Nathaniel de Rothschild; and in 1977, it commemorated the official visit to the Médoc of Her Majesty Queen Elizabeth, the Queen Mother.

THE CHOICE OF ARTISTS

The contract drawn up between each artist and Baron Philippe gave both parties a degree of independence. The maker of each label had carte blanche to paint whatever the theme inspired — the vine, the pleasure of drinking, or the idea of the ram. Baron Philippe, on the other hand, had carte blanche to reject any design, however famous the artist might be, that did not fit the Mouton style.

On the question of payment, the arrangement was equally unconventional: No money was to change hands, but the artist agreed to take cases of Mouton Rothschild of the year he had illustrated, and additional cases from any other year he wanted.

Baron Philippe's choice of artists has always been eclectic: from 1946 to 1954, he approached only artists who were also personal friends — Jean Hugo, Jean Cocteau, Arnulf, Léonor Fini. In 1955, however, there was an important new development: the great Georges Braque agreed to design a label. Taking their cue from him, several other internationally known artists — including Dali, Miró, Chagall — contributed designs in the years that followed.

Nonetheless, the labels of certain years bear witness to a willingness to take a risk: On several occasions the commission was given to painters of stature who were less familiar to the general public — Matta and Pierre Alechinsky, for example — or to artists already established in media other than painting, including the sculptors César, Richard Lippold, and Henry Moore.

The year 1973, when Mouton Rothschild was officially proclaimed a *Premier Cru*, was also the year of Picasso's death. One of his paintings, already in the possession of the Mouton Museum, illustrated the label for that year.

Since 1974, there has been increasingly frequent participation by artists from abroad:

Andy Warhol signs his label

Americans like Robert Motherwell and Andy Warhol; the Canadian painter Riopelle, and the Japanese Domoto. This increasingly international element in the labels reflects an ever-growing interest in Bordeaux wines and the worldwide success of Mouton Rothschild.

A CASE FOR EACH YEAR

This collection of paintings and drawings casts a new and sometimes unexpected light on the work of those artists who have illustrated the Mouton Rothschild labels. It is the first time the originals have left the archives at Mouton.

Despite the unifying influence of the commission, the organizers of the present exhibition were faced with real difficulties: First, there was the problem of presenting in sequence works so widely different in style, technique, and above all in size, ranging from a few square inches to several square feet. Second, two works were missing: Jean Cocteau's drawing for 1947 had been lost, and the Kandinsky lent by his widow for the 1971 label was now in the possession of the Louvre. Finally, the two commemorative years, 1953 and 1977, had not been illustrated by painters.

It was therefore essential to try to find a common denominator that would accommodate the individuality of each work and allow it to "breathe," to impose its own rhythm. The solution proved to be display cases, reproduced here on the page facing the works themselves.

In the exhibition, these cases create a three-dimensional space in which, against different colored backgrounds, the original work can be related to supporting documents (the printed label, photographs, press clippings, and even personal mementos of the painter) that may help to put them in context.

The cases for the years 1953, 1971, and 1977 may not be works of art, but they are at least works of craft, with their own charm.

Various sizes have been used for the labels, ranging from 32 x 41 centimeters to 78 x 108 centimeters.

The Paintings

[1924 Jean Carlu]

1945 Victory Year (Philippe Jullian)

1946 Jean Hugo

1947 Jean Cocteau

1948 Marie Laurencin

1949 Dignimont

1950 Arnulf

1951 Marcel Vertès

1952 Léonor Fini

1953 Centenary Year

1954 Jean Carzou

1955 Georges Braque

1956 Pavel Tchelitchew

1957 André Masson

1958 Salvador Dali

1959 Richard Lippold

1960 Jacques Villon

1961 Georges Mathieu

1962 Matta

1963 Bernard Dufour

1964 Henry Moore

1965 Dorothea Tanning

1966 Pierre Alechinsky

1967 César

1968 Bona

1969 Joan Miró

1970 Marc Chagall

1971 Wassily Kandinsky

1972 Serge Poliakoff

1973 Pablo Picasso

1974 Robert Motherwell

1975 Andy Warhol

1976 Pierre Soulages

1977 Tribute to H.M. the Queen Mother

1978 Jean-Paul Riopelle

1979 Hisao Domoto

1980 Hans Hartung

1981 Arman

Born in 1900, Carlu came from a family of archi-tects, his brother Jacques being responsible for the Palais de Chaillot in Paris. After a short time at the Ecole des Beaux-Arts, he began to special-ize, at the age of seventeen, in poster design.

In 1918 he was sufficiently well established to be named Designer of the Year by a panel of judges headed by the famous graphic designer Cappiello. The same day Carlu lost his right arm in a road accident. Although this meant a long period of retraining and readjustment, he refused to let this loss prevent him from continuing in his chosen career. There is an echo of the tragedy in the image of the hand that often recurs in his later work.

Based on what at the time was highly original imagery — the profile, the mask, and the obses-sively repeated hand — his work as a poster designer developed in three areas in particular: First, political commitment; this was focused from as early as 1930 on the peace movement (*Le Désarmement,* 1932) and the struggle against National Socialism (*Stop Hitler Now,* 1940). He produced the latter in the United States, where he was resident from 1940 to 1953. Second, the expression, in poster form, of the dominant artistic movements of the day: Cubism (as in the label for Mouton Rothschild 1924) and Surreal-ism, under the influence of André Breton and Yves Tanguy, as in the *Reichold Chemicals* poster. Finally, an impressive series of technical innova-tions: the introduction of photomontage (the poster of the film *Atlantis* by Pabst in 1932), the use of three-dimensional elements in poster design (*La Grande Maison de Blanc,* 1933), and the use of electric lightbulbs in poster composition (*Luminograph,* 1937).

For fifty years Carlu's popularity as a commercial artist has remained undimmed. He was one of the first graphic designers to recognize the value of clean line and strong color in fixing a brand image in the mind of the buying public; these same qualities give Carlu's posters their power as works of art.

Gouache
Signed at lower right
27.7 x 37.8 cm

7

Victory Year (PHILIPPE JULLIAN)

In 1945, to commemorate the Allied victory, Baron Philippe de Rothschild conceived the idea of decorating the Mouton Rothschild label with the reproduction of a work of art: in this instance a symbolic design was chosen to celebrate the coming of peace and the return to normal life.

He commissioned this work from a young artist, Philippe Jullian, in those days entirely unknown. Jullian was a gifted designer and was later to become a successful playwright and essayist. From the various sketches he submitted, Baron Philippe chose the V for Victory, with which Churchill for five years had rallied the free world and the code sign also of the French Resistance, transmitted from London in Morse code throughout the Occupation.

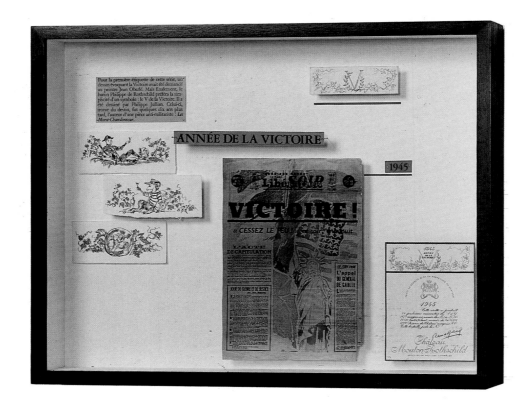

Ink and gouache
(three other drawings, also ink and gouache)
3.2 x 10.2 cm

The first professional painter to illustrate a label for Mouton Rothschild was Jean Hugo, a direct descendant of the great Victor Hugo. Born in 1894, he worked first as a stage designer, coming to the attention of the general public in 1921 with his costumes for Jean Cocteau's *Les Mariés de la Tour Eiffel*. By 1924, he was working with the great Russian dancer Léonide Massine on scenery for his ballets. He later worked again with Cocteau, providing the sets for an adaptation of *Romeo and Juliet*.

A close friend of two of the leading novelists of the day, Raymond Radiguet and Paul Morand, of the composer Georges Auric and the painter Roger de La Fresnaye, all of whom he captured in drawings with striking success, he was also a popular figure at Parisian parties between the wars, devising masks and fancy-dress costumes.

Throughout the thirties he became increasingly involved in the theater, designing sets at the Comédie Française for Racine's *Phèdre* and for *Anthony and Cleopatra*. He also illustrated several books, in particular *Climats* by André Maurois. At the same time his work as an oil painter and watercolorist gained him a reputation as a master of the miniature. He now lives in the south of France, and has recently published his memoirs, *Before I Forget*.

For the 1946 label, Jean Hugo took his inspiration from the story of the Flood: the dove with the olive branch in its beak, returning to the Ark—a symbol of the first year of peace.

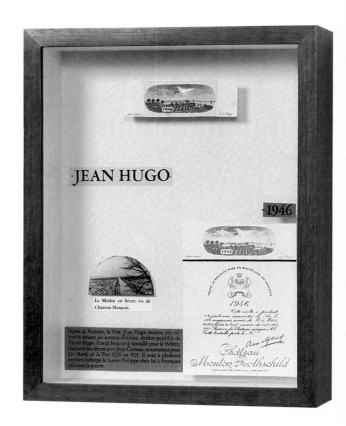

Lavis inédit

1946

de J. Hugo

Ink and gouache
Signed at lower center
3.3 x 6.3 cm

Novelist, dramatist, filmmaker, painter and designer, but first and foremost a poet, Jean Cocteau (1889–1963) belonged, in his love of formal perfection and the myths of Greece and Rome, to the great French classical tradition. He can also be called a Surrealist for the desire evident in his poetry to go beyond the bounds of reason, and in his passion to unsettle, or indeed flout, existing artistic and moral convention. As Diaghilev used to say, "Jean, étonne-moi! (astonish me!)"

An active force in modern art of every kind, he made a considerable contribution in his writing, particularly about de Chirico, Picasso, and Modigliani, to the understanding of con-temporary painting. He also worked with the composers of the *Groupe des Six* on the highly experimental *Les Mariés de la Tour Eiffel*.

Cocteau was the great star of Parisian society, transforming dinner party conversation with the brilliance of his wit, suddenly, floating ideas either too fragile or too outrageous ever to reach the printed page. As he himself cryptically observed, "Those who can, will understand: I am a lie that always tells the truth."

Nevertheless, he was no mere provider of instant and perishable entertainment; he also produced a vast output of inspired work in many different fields: novels, *Thomas l'imposteur*, in 1922, which he illustrated himself, and *Les Enfants terribles*, 1929; plays, *La Voix humaine*, 1930, *La Machine infernale*, 1934, and *Les Parents terribles*, 1938; films, *Le Sang d'un poète*, 1930, *L'Eternel retour*, 1943, and *La Belle et la Bête*, 1946; published poetry, from *L'Ange Heurtebise*, 1925, to *Requiem*, 1963; and finally graphic designs.

Paradoxically for a mind of such versatility, he returned throughout his career almost obses-sively to the same profile of a youth that he used on the Mouton label for 1947. The model for that profile was Jean Marais, then starring in the first performance of Cocteau's play *L'Aigle a deux têtes*. The original drawing having been lost, it was Marais, a painter as well as an actor and a lifelong friend of Cocteau, who was invited to make this copy for the present exhibition.

Pour
Jean Cocteau
★ Récolte 1947
Jean Marais

Les plantes et les animaux
Nous enseignent notre ligne
Lorsque tu plantes ma vigne
Je récolte le vin des mots
Jean Cocteau

Ink, after a drawing by Jean Cocteau
20 x 29 cm
Signed by Jean Marais

13

Marie Laurencin (1885–1956) is widely known for her romantic, soft-toned images. Nevertheless, she experienced the adventure of Cubism very much at first hand. Through her relationship with Apollinaire, celebrated in her picture *Apollinaire and his friends* (1909), she was closely involved in the avant-garde movements of the period.

Influenced at the beginning of her career by the stylizations of the Cubists and by Picasso's work of the same period, her paintings soon moved towards a more decorative manner inspired by the "Nabis," the group of figurative painters that had included Bonnard and Maurice Denis. She also provided the sets for Poulenc's ballet *Les Biches* in 1924, and numerous book illustrations, including editions of Gide and Lewis Carroll.

Not a member of any school or definable system, her real originality lies in her talent as a colorist, marked by the use of very subtle tones; and in her sometimes affected naïveté and love of graceful adolescent faces, as in the label for 1948.

Ink and watercolor
Signed at left
13 x 32 cm

A Parisian painter, André Dignimont (1891–1965) frequently exhibited at the Salon d'Automne and was closely connected with the world of contemporary writing, largely through his friendship with Francis Carco. A designer and watercolorist, he devoted his gifts in particular to revitalizing the art of book illustration, and was particularly successful in his work for well-known texts like Perrault's *Contes*, Colette's *Ingénue libertine*, Margaret Mitchell's *Gone with the Wind*, and Francis Carco's *Perversité*.

His painting also reveals a love of popular pastimes and amusements, cafés dansants, the world of prostitutes and cabarets. The same love of life is present in his drawing for the Mouton label, which shows a table in the garden of a country tavern; it is a measure of his accuracy and passion for detail that both the wine bottles and the glasses are of a typically Bordeaux design.

The year 1949 is one of the best vintages of the century.

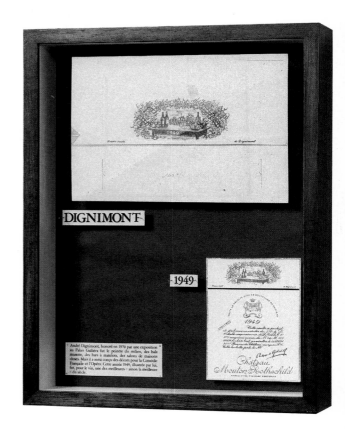

Dessin inédit · · · · · · · · · · · · · · · de Dignimont

Pencil and gouache
Signed at lower right
16 x 24 cm

Born in 1921 in Monaco, Arnulf studied at the Ecole des Beaux-Arts in Paris. He won the Grand Prix de Rome for engraving in 1950. The label for Mouton Rothschild dates from the same year: his skill as an engraver comes through in the clarity of line and the rigorous perspective in which he sets the symbol of the Ram.

Arnulf's interest in pre-Columbian art took him to South America, where he lived from 1957 to 1966, occupying various cultural posts and working at the same time on stained glass and fresco painting. In 1967, he returned to France to teach design, first in Nice and then in Paris. He has exhibited in several French cities, provided murals for public buildings, and illustrated various deluxe editions.

In contrast to the economy of design evident in the Mouton label, his later work has developed into a more elaborate and florid style, combining human figures with plants, rocks, and animals in vigorous movement.

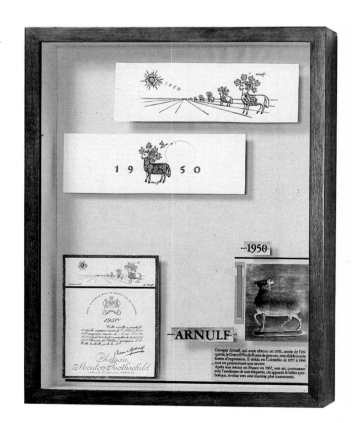

Ink and gouache
Signed at upper right
6.6 x 20 cm
(A second drawing, ink and gouache, same size,
signed between the Ram's feet)

Vertès (1896–1961), Austrian-born, began his career as a poster designer in Vienna before settling in Paris. He established his reputation with a book of drawings, *Dancing*, published in Vienna in 1922, and was a keen-eyed observer of the twenties. Fascinated by the movement and grace of the female body, he captured it in quick, sensuous, and telling strokes of the pen.

Using a number of techniques, including lithography, engraving, and dry-point, he immediately attracted the attention of publishers, who from 1925 onwards increasingly employed him as an illustrator. He was much in demand by writers of the day for deluxe editions of their work: *La Semaine secrète de Vénus* (1925) and *Les Jeux du demi-jour* (1926) by Mac Orlan, *La Vagabonde* (1927) and *Chéri* (1929) by Colette, *L'Europe galante* (1927) by Paul Morand, and *Belle de jour* (1929) by Joseph Kessel.

He also illustrated works by authors of the previous generation, including Verlaine, Apollinaire (*Oeuvres erotiques*, 1934) Pierre Louÿs, and Courteline. The innocent sensuality of his work is well expressed in the shepherd and shepherdess he provided for the label of 1951.

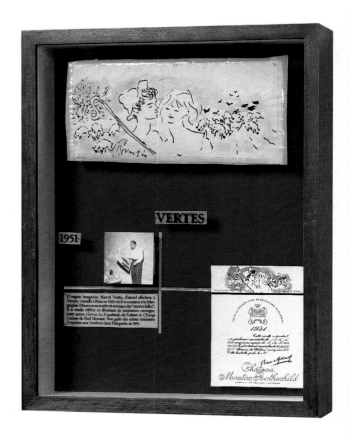

Ink and watercolor
Signed at lower left
10.5 x 23 cm

21

Italian by birth, Léonor Fini, born in 1918, was influenced in her youth by the Pre-Raphaelites and by Aubrey Beardsley, leading her to concentrate on technical precision and an elegance of line that can at times become mannered. Her passion for the German Romantics led her quite naturally to join the Surrealist movement, which brought to her work a rather mysterious eroticism and certain recurring themes: bisexual figures (*Stryges Amaouri*, 1948), animals with human heads, like the "She-Ram" on the 1952 label, and dream landscapes like *La Terre rouge* of 1961.

This work, drawing on the subconscious mind for its ambiguity and depth, was to find a new direction in stage design for the opera and theater: Wagner's *Tannhäuser* (1963) at the Paris Opera, Anouilh's version of *The Importance of Being Earnest*, by Oscar Wilde (1954), and *The Council of Love*, by Panizza (1969) at the Théâtre de Paris.

In 1968, she illustrated an edition of *Histoire d'O*, the erotic best-seller by Pauline Réage. Much loved by Parisian society, Fini carries with her a taste for extravagance and mystery.

Black and red ink
A note in pencil, "Dessin
inédit de Léonor Fini,"
at lower center
32 x 23.4 cm

Centenary Year

On May 11, 1853, Baron Nathaniel de Rothschild signed the contract that made him proprietor of Château Brane-Mouton, and immediately renamed it Château Mouton Rothschild. To commemorate the event, his great-grandson Baron Philippe de Rothschild dedicated the 1953 vintage to his memory; the label bears his portrait.

Below are the original title-deeds to the estate.

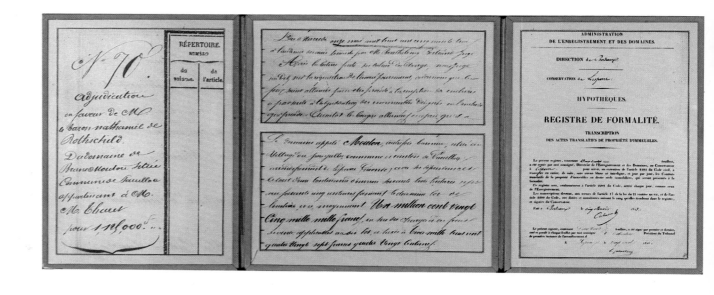

Le Baron Henri
1872-1947

·Le Baron Philippe·

Le Baron Nathaniel
1812-1870

Le Baron James
1844-1881

·1953·

·ANNÉE DU CENTENAIRE·

Jean Carzou, born in 1907 of Armenian parents, studied architecture before he turned to painting. Despite a successful first exhibition in Paris in 1939, his work became known only after 1945, and in 1949 he won the Prix de la Peinture Contemporaine. He exhibited in Switzerland in 1951 and again in Paris in 1958–1959, with a series of pictures painted in Venice.

At the same time, he was making a reputation for himself as a stage designer, both for the theater and for ballet: *Les Indes galantes* (1952); *Le Loup* for Roland Petit (1953); *Giselle* at the Paris Opera (1954, the year in which he designed the label); *Athalie* (1955) at the Comédie Française; and *La Périchole* at the Théâtre de Paris (1970).

His work relies for its impact on the contrast between the rigorous geometry of his spatial construction and the irrational tangle of lines with which he represents his figures. From this, he creates a personal poetic universe that transcends contemporary reality; whether he is painting a townscape, a railway, or an industrial scene, he endows it with an element of fantasy, using color —sometimes somber, sometimes radiant—to evoke a nightmare or a dream, as in *Apocalypse* (1956) and *Le Paradis terrestre* (1959).

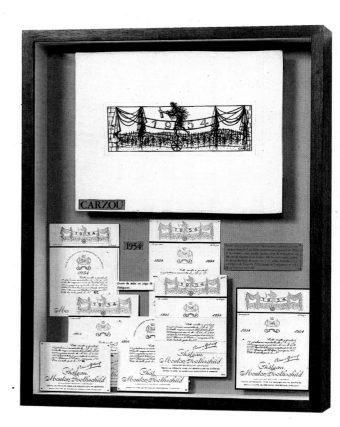

Ink, gouache, and gold paint
Signed at lower right and dated: 1953
22.5 x 28.8 cm

27

The first painter of international stature to illustrate a Mouton Rothschild label, Georges Braque (1882–1963), the son of a Le Havre house painter, was expected to follow in his father's footsteps. Very soon, however, he broke away to study art, inspired at first by the Impressionist tradition. After coming to Paris in 1900, he was involved in the brief phenomenon of Fauvism (*Le Port de l'Estaque*, 1906); however, the Cézanne exhibition at the Salon d'Automne in 1907 and Picasso's *Demoiselles d'Avignon* of the same year were to determine the future direction of his work. Building on Cézanne's principle of diagrammatic construction, he used it, as did Picasso, as the basis of a real revolution in painting: Cubism.

"What fascinated me personally and what was the main thrust of Cubism was the feeling of a new dimension in space" . . . space out of which he and Picasso were to make the very stuff of their paintings, rejecting perspective, however sacrosanct, juxtaposing in the same plane images of an object seen from different angles, exploding the original object into simple geometrical forms (*Les Instruments de musique*, 1908, and *La Table à la pipe*, 1912).

The years between 1909 and 1914, a time of close collaboration with Picasso, saw Braque's work develop from Analytical Cubism to Synthetic Cubism, from landscape to neutral-colored still life. In 1913, with the invention of collage, he reverted to brighter colors.

Seriously wounded in the First World War, he resumed work still dedicated to the aesthetic ideas of Cubism. The human form, virtually absent from his work until that time, made its appearance in his series of *Canephores*, 1922–1927, and in paintings of nudes and bathing figures. He returned to landscape with *La Plage de Dieppe*, 1929, and his still lifes of this period, with their full curves and opulent harmonies of dark color, seemed to vibrate with intense light (*Le Chevalet*, 1938, *Tabouret, Vase, Palette*, 1939).

The publication of his *Notebooks* in 1947 was hailed as an event of major importance. His sculptures, stained glass windows, and his work in jewelry, all added to his reputation.

The design for the 1955 label, though characteristic, is one of the most literal interpretations of the theme.

Ink and watercolor
Signed at lower right and
dated at lower left: 1955
13.3 x 10.3 cm

PAVEL TCHELITCHEW

Born in Moscow of an aristocratic family, Tchelitchew (1898–1957) was studying drawing in Kiev at the time of the Revolution. He then traveled through Turkey, Bulgaria, and Austria and spent three years in Berlin (1920–1923), which gave him the opportunity of working as a stage designer. He settled in Paris in 1923, where his work attracted the attention of Gertrude Stein, among others. It was there that he reacted against abstract art, contributing to the Neo-Romantic exhibition of 1926.

In 1928, he designed the sets and costumes for Diaghilev's ballet *Ode*, and then illustrated René Crevel's *L'Esprit contre la raison*. At the same time, he was becoming closely involved with the Surrealist group. When the war broke out, he was in New York with Yves Tanguy, Max Ernst, and André Breton. In 1942, Charles Henry Ford's magazine *View* published an important article on his work, analyzing his ability, like that of Dali, to capture a violent and fantastic vision within the disciplines of classical drawing.

His label, *La Tache de vin*, is one of his last works.

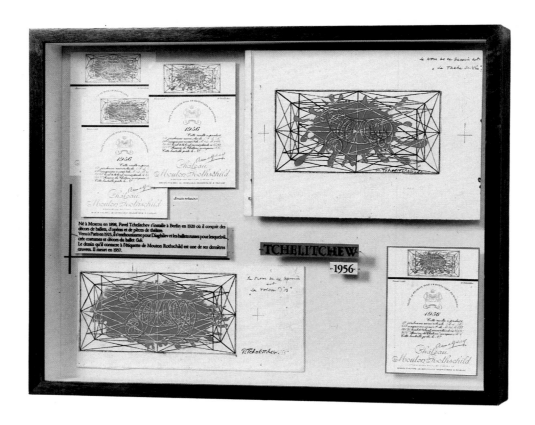

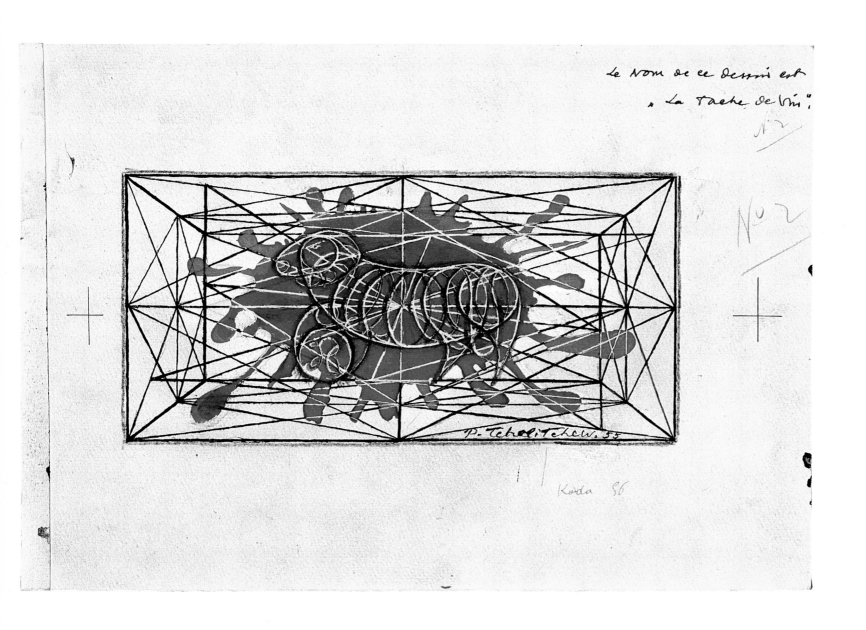

Gouache
At top right, the title "La tache de vin";
signed and dated: 55, at lower right
18.7 x 26.2 cm

ANDRÉ MASSON

After a brief Cubist period, André Masson, born in 1896, became an early adherent of Surrealism, which had a profound and lasting impact on his work. In his drawing, he applied the technique of automatic writing to liberate the subconscious mind through freedom of movement, producing ambiguous, fragmented shapes, a tangle of lines made more emphatic by violent and contrasting colors. André Breton said of his work: "Eroticism is the keystone."

In 1929, he broke with the Surrealists, describing himself from then on as "a Surrealist dissident" (*Entretiens*, 1958). He spent long periods in Catalonia (*Tauromachies, Massacres*, 1932–1936), and the Spanish Civil War turned the natural violence of his work increasingly toward a darker, more tragic form of expressionism.

From 1941 to 1944, Masson lived in the United States, where he was an important influence on the theory and inspiration of the Abstract Expressionist movement in America. In 1947 he returned to France to live in Provence, where his work came to some extent under the influence of both Cézanne and Matisse. He also worked as a stage designer, notably on *Hamlet* in 1946 and *Tête d'or* in 1959, both for Jean-Louis Barrault.

A friend of Malraux, he illustrated his novel *Les Conquérants* and was commissioned by Malraux in 1966 to paint the ceiling of the Théâtre de l'Odéon in Paris.

For the label of 1957, Masson chose to dramatize the idea of intoxication in a work in which the branches of the living vine become confused with the contours of the human body in a celebration of absolute contentment: drunken slumber in a vineyard.

Gouache
Signed at lower right and dated at lower left: 1957
11.7 x 21.4 cm

33

A devout Surrealist, not only in his work but in his everyday life, Salvador Dali remains a living legend and a highly original artist of great technical brilliance. Dali was born in Catalonia in 1904, and while studying fine art in Madrid in 1921, he discovered de Chirico's "Metaphysical Surrealism." This led him, when he arrived in Paris, to join the Surrealist movement, of which he was soon to become one of the leading figures.

In his collaboration with Luis Buñuel on the films *Un Chien andalou* (1929) and *L'Age d'or* (1930), in the work shown at his first Parisian exhibition (1929, with a catalogue by André Breton), and in his urge to make the hallucinatory world of the Surrealists a part of daily life in the way he dressed and behaved, it is possible to see one constant element: a combination of strict, sometimes academic, discipline with extraordinary and alarming images — often with strong sexual overtones, as seen in his famous soft watches — dredged directly from the subconscious.

His anarchic sense of humor led him at times to parody famous works of art — *The Angelus* by Millet, Vermeer's *The Lacemaker* — and even historical characters such as William Tell, Voltaire, Wagner, or Lenin, who appear in his works as popular legend has imagined them, but cut down to comic size in weird and fantastic surroundings. He himself has defined his view of the world as "paranoid-critical."

His marriage to Gala in 1931, until then the inseparable companion of the poet Paul Eluard, brought about a rift with the Surrealists on what were described at the time as political grounds. She remained his constant muse and manager. Dali went to the United States in 1940, prompting André Breton to compose the malicious anagram of his name "Avida Dollars" (Greedy for Dollars).

Alternately entertaining and horrifying, erotic and devout, ranging from academic pastiche to near-insanity, the works of Salvador Dali flout all accepted definitions in headlong pursuit of his current train of thought or association of ideas. The general public, even those with no interest in art, continue to find it fascinating — a tribute to his own amazing flair for outrage and carefully orchestrated publicity. As he once said in an interview with the BBC: "I am not a great painter, not a great businessman, but a genius."

It is paradoxical that Surrealism should have found in him so lucid a prophet and advocate.

Ink and gold paint
Signed in the drawing, and dated: 1952; a note at the top:
"Aussi très bon". 4.3 x 7.5 cm
(Two other drawings, ink and gold paint, both signed in
the drawing and dated: 1952)

RICHARD LIPPOLD

An American sculptor of German origin, Lippold was born in 1915 and began his career as an industrial designer. In the early forties he devised the means of expression that established his reputation in the United States: linear sculpture, organizing space in a mesh of brass, nickel, or copper wires, spreading outwards from opposing poles to form expanding geometrical figures. Lippold defines his aesthetic theory in the following terms: "Only metal wire, in my opinion, allows sculpture to express the conquest of space, and space is the basic raw material of the present age."

His first large-scale work was *Full Moon* (1950), which was immediately bought by the Museum of Modern Art in New York. Another work on the same monumental scale, *The Sun* (1953), in gold wire, went to the Metropolitan Museum. These sculptures were followed by *Orpheus and Apollo* (1962) for the great hall of Lincoln Center, and *Flight* (1963) for the Pan-American Building, both in New York. He also provided a canopy for the Cathedral of Saint Mary in San Francisco. Lippold's technique, a creative use of metallic structures, gives this spatial geometry a great lightness and an aura of modernity.

For the label of 1959 he has managed to translate into his own abstract language the color of the wine and the rows of growing vines.

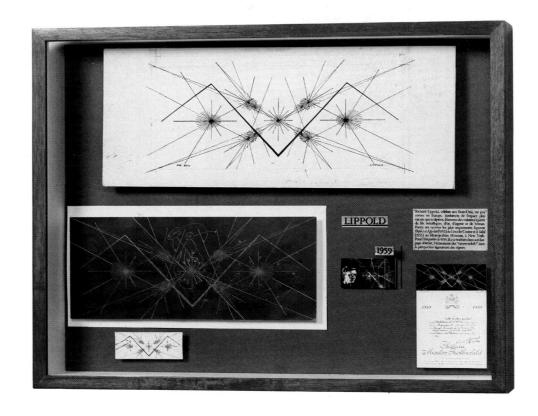

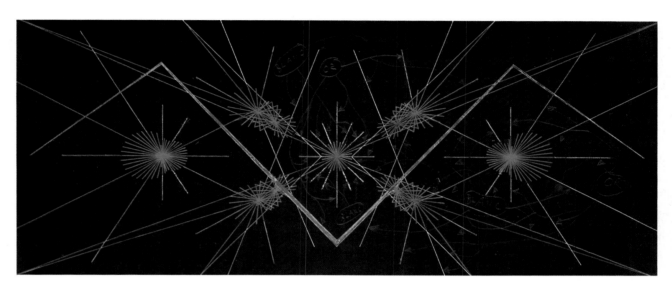

Watercolor: Artist's notes to the printer in pencil at bottom
Signed at lower right; a note on the left: "For Ero"
20.7 x 51 cm

1960   JACQUES VILLON

Born Gaston Duchamp, Jacques Villon (1875–1963) was the brother of the sculptor Raymond Duchamp-Villon and of the painter Marcel Duchamp. Having moved to Paris in 1894, he started work as a newspaper cartoonist, and also drew realistic sketches of Parisian street life. From 1911 onwards his studio in Puteaux became a meeting place where Cubist painters like Gleizes, Metzinger, Léger, and Picabia worked, exchanged ideas, and discussed the mathematical and geometrical concepts that came to fruition in 1912 in the *Section d'or* exhibition organized by Albert Gleizes.

In 1913 Villon's work was exhibited at the historic Armory Show in New York, which shocked the American public into a sudden awareness of new developments in modern art in Europe. At this stage, Villon's painting became unashamedly non-representational. Combining the architectural rigor of Cubism with his own fascination for the problems of light and color, it found expression in abstract compositions of flat areas of color, arranged in geometrical forms (*Soldats en marche*, 1913). In the late twenties, now firmly established in the United States, thanks to the support of the art critic Walter Pach, Villon tried to apply his own personal style of painting to traditional forms like the portrait (*Homme dessinant*, 1935; *Portrait de Marcel Duchamp*, 1951) and the landscape (*Les Moissons*, 1943). The Carnegie Prize in 1950 and the Grand Prix at the Venice Biennale in 1956 came in recognition of Jacques Villon's work as innovator, painter, exquisite colorist, and one of the masters of Cubism.

In his label for Mouton Rothschild 1960, he contrasts the movement of the birds with the static geometry of the vines.

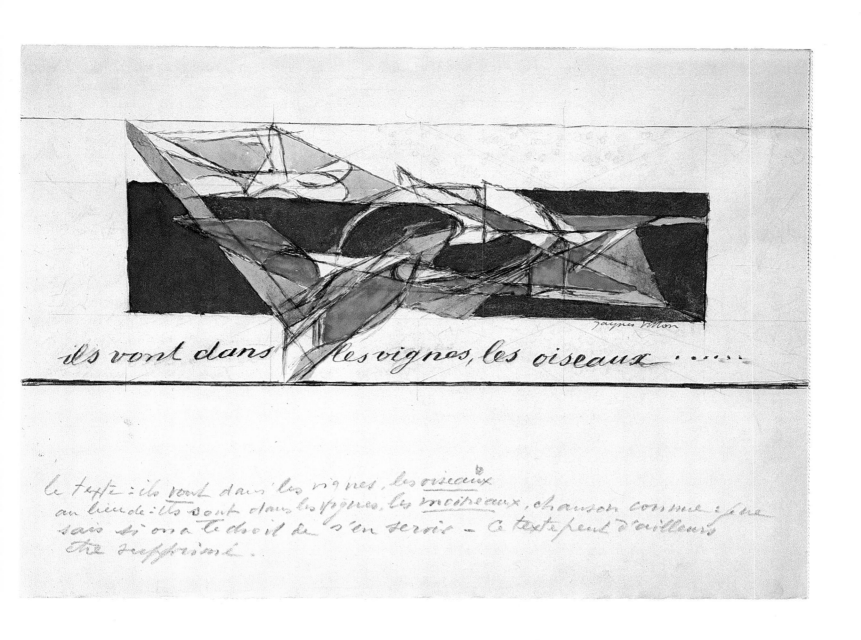

ils vont dans les vignes, les oiseaux ……

Watercolor and gouache
Signed at lower right
25.8 x 35.8 cm

39

Hailed by Malraux — "At last, calligraphy in the West!" — Georges Mathieu, born in 1921, began painting in the early forties, settling in Paris in 1947. Condemning what he called cold geometrical abstraction, he proclaimed himself the founder of "Lyrical Abstraction," the principles of which had been revealed to him by two painters in particular, Wols and Hartung.

Every painter can be said to have his own language; Mathieu would go further and claim to have invented a complete system of signs, a kind of imaginative semaphore to communicate our primitive inner violence. "Painting," as he says, "has to be acted out." The act of painting becomes a wild struggle with the canvas, one that Mathieu sometimes demonstrates in the presence of an audience, producing at bewildering speed huge canvases of violent color and tormented composition (*La Bataille de Bouvines*, 1954, and *Paris, capitale des arts*, 1965). Exhibitionism is therefore a central element in his attitude to painting, expressed in a series of pamphlets or manifestos like *D'Aristote à l'abstraction lyrique* (1959) and *Au-delà du tachisme* (1963). His study of technique inevitably led him to Japan, the home of calligraphy, and he enjoyed a considerable success there in 1957.

Mathieu has also been concerned with re-establishing closer links between the painter and the modern world, and has accepted commissions from several large companies, making drawings for Pierre Cardin, designing posters for Air France, and providing advertisements for furniture manufacturers and jewelers.

The explosive energy of the 1961 label is typical of his work.

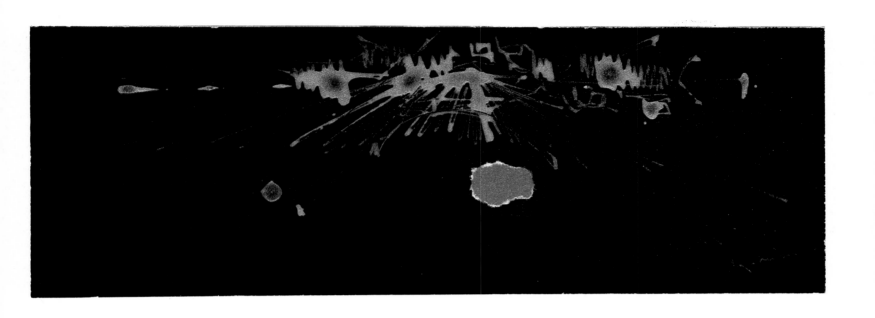

Oil and collage
Signed at lower right
7 x 20.1 cm

Born of Chilean parents in 1912, Roberto Matta Echaurren, known as Matta, worked first as an architect with Le Corbusier. He joined the Surrealist group in 1935 and made his name as a painter with his *Morphologies psychologiques* in 1938.

Matta's Surrealism tended not so much towards the spontaneous expression of a personal vision as to a conscious refraction of reality, split into almost geological strata. The best-known work of this period is *Inscape*, painted in 1939, an escape from reality into the inner world.

He spent the war years in the United States, where he came very much under the influence of Yves Tanguy and Marcel Duchamp, and returned to Paris in 1948 to paint a large-scale fresco for the UNESCO building, *Trois Etres — Constellations face au feu*, 1958. After the war, in the face of mounting violence and the increased pressures of modern life, Matta turned to the portrayal of a mechanized world, peopled with creatures that were half-robots, half-clowns.

In the 1962 Mouton label the harsh skeletal outlines of the vines are balanced by the gentler legend: "*Son tendre velouté séduit les plus rebelles*" (Its velvet tenderness will melt the hardest heart).

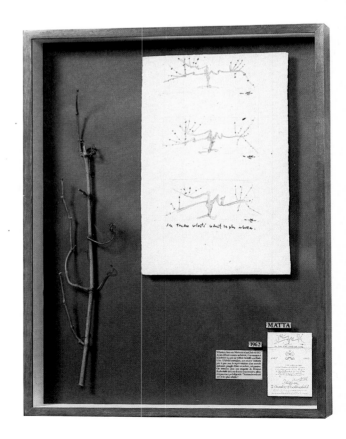

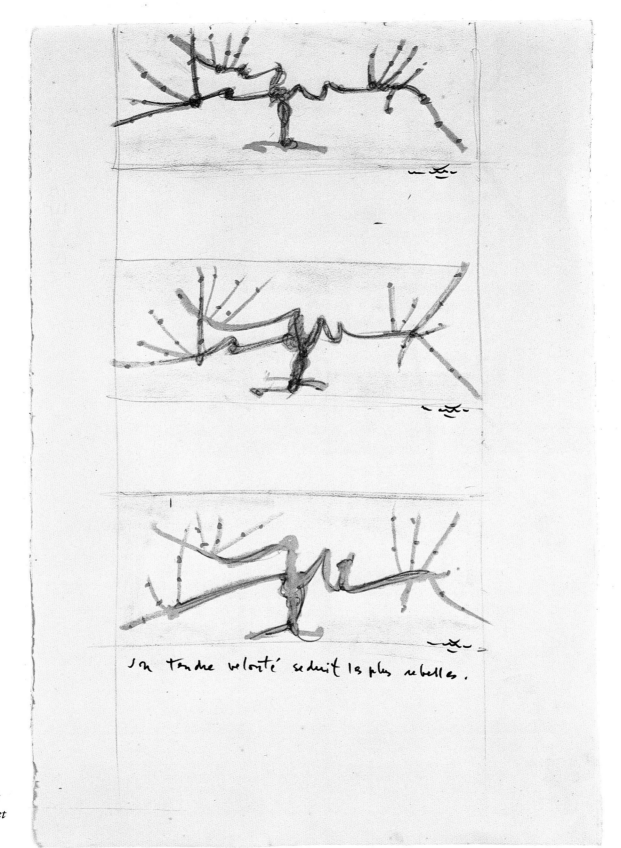

Son tendre volonté seduit la plus rebelle.

Ink and gouache
Three drawings signed at
lower right, on single sheet
50 x 33.3 cm

Born in 1922, Bernard Dufour completed his training as an agricultural engineer before becoming a painter in 1945. His work was first shown at the Salon de Mai, 1948, where it was widely praised, and subsequently at Pierre Loeb's gallery until the latter's death in 1964. His son, Albert Loeb, presented his paintings in New York in 1959, and in London in 1960. In 1964, Georges Bernier (then director of the Galerie l'Oeil) showed Dufour's paintings at the Venice Biennale. In 1977, he took part in the *Guillotine et Peinture* exhibition at the Musée d'Art Moderne de la Ville de Paris, and since then has regularly been in exhibitions with Pierre Nahon at the Galerie Beaubourg.

After a nonfigurative period painting abstract landscape, he began to turn, in 1960, towards more representational painting: female nudes, self-portraits with sad, staring eyes; a mood of eroticism but always softened by a reflective haze; an imprecision of line, tricks of light, mirror-images, reality seen in a dream.

The sensual element in his work is evident in this design for the Mouton label of 1963, a naked girl with grapes, and the legend: "*Ainsi quand des raisins j'ai sucé la clarté*" (As, when I sucked the lustre from the grapes . . .).

Watercolor
Signed at upper left
and dated: 1963
13.2 x 10 cm

45

Henry Moore was born in 1898, the son of a Yorkshire miner. He studied first in Leeds and then at the Royal College of Art in London, returning there to teach between 1926 and 1939. His monumental sculpture immediately attracted widespread attention in the late twenties, as did his first exhibition in 1928. After 1930, his work was regularly exhibited with that of the Surrealists — in London, 1936; Mexico, 1940; New York, 1942. He was also influenced by both Brancusi and pre-Columbian art.

From these beginnings Henry Moore went on to achieve a way of representing the human figure that is absolutely characteristic: molding elementary shapes, simplifying forms to give them a universal quality and to express primitive images of fertility or power. "What interests me most deeply is the human body," he wrote. He succeeds in bringing real life to these heavy silhouettes, tunneling through them, and creating deep areas of empty space within the mass of his material. During the Second World War, he made a series of drawings of sleeping figures in the London Underground, then used as an air-raid shelter.

Henry Moore won the Grand Prix at the Venice Biennale in 1948, and is represented in the world's greatest museums, as well as in the public parks of many capital cities. He ranks among the most important sculptors of our time.

His drawing for the 1964 label, three chalices cradled in cupped hands, evokes a mood of solemn ritual.

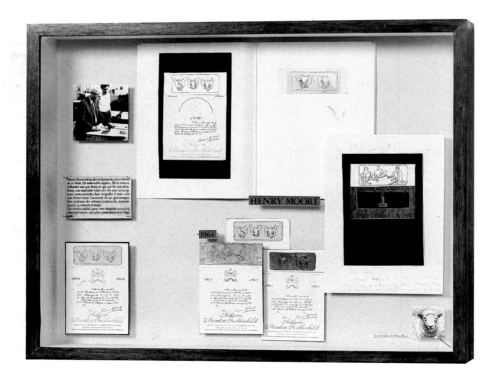

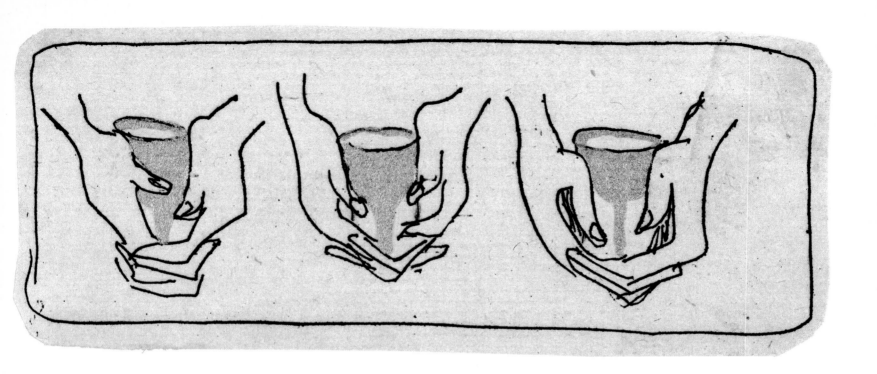

Ink and gold paint
3.3 x 8 cm
(Two other drawings, ink and gold paint)

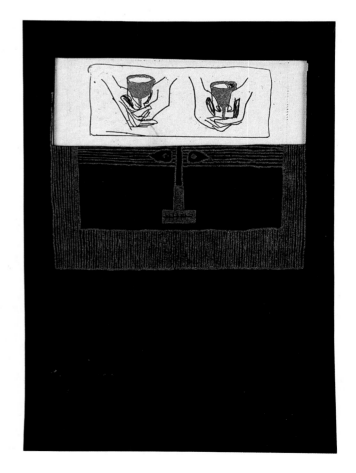

The American artist Dorothea Tanning was born in 1912, and discovered Surrealism in 1936 at the time of the great exhibition at the Museum of Modern Art in New York. In 1942 she met Max Ernst, and four years later married him, living and working with him in close collaboration, first in the United States and later in France.

Always faithful to the tenets of Surrealism, Dorothea Tanning returns in her work to certain characteristic images: monstrous flowers and strangely sinister, waiflike girls in rags, as in *Children's Games* (1942) and *Eine kleine Nächtmusik* (1944).

She has worked in a great many fields, creating stage designs for Giraudoux's *Judith* (directed by Jean-Louis Barrault, 1961); ballet designs for Balanchine's *Bayou*, at the New York City Ballet; etchings for Alain Bosquet's *Paroles peintes* (1959); and copperplate engravings for André Pieyre de Mandiargues' *La Marée* (1970).

While not possessing the hallucinatory precision of her earlier work, her saraband of little rams for the 1965 label is typical of her work in its fluid, dreamlike sense of movement.

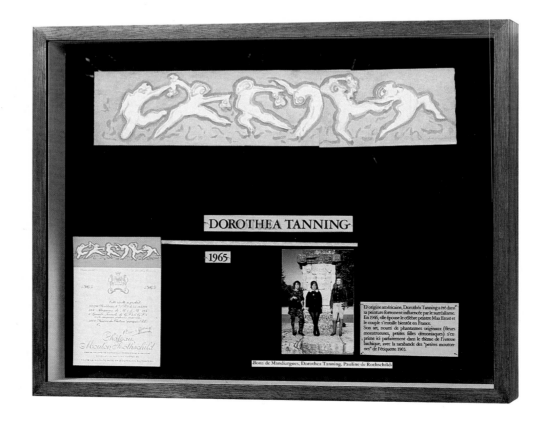

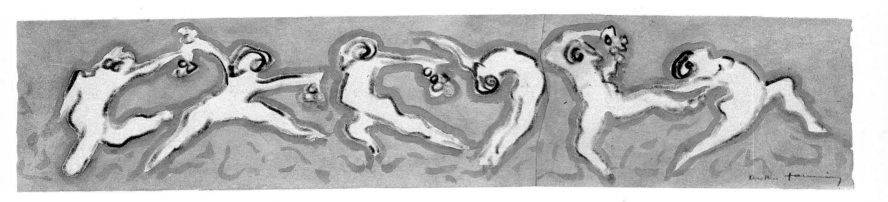

Watercolor and pencil
Signed at lower right
8.4 x 40 cm

A painter, designer, and poet from Belgium, Pierre Alechinsky was born in 1927. In 1948 he was one of the founders, with the poet Christian Dotremont, of the Cobra Group (COpenhagen, BRussels, Amsterdam). The group set out to transcend the antagonism then existing between abstract and figurative artists to create a style of baroque expressionism in direct challenge to the Paris school of painters.

Nonetheless, for all its radical intentions, Alechinsky's work is also part of the continuing tradition of Paul Klee, and to some extent of Surrealism, in his sense of mystery and his reliance on the spontaneity of automatic drawing. In his canvases, with their organic and exuberant movement, a world of grotesque figures jostle endlessly in a state of flux.

Settling in Paris in 1951, Alechinsky has spent time in both the United States and Japan, has made a film on Oriental calligraphy, and has published numerous books of poetry, including *Idéotraces* and *Roue libre*.

The freedom and imagination with which he treats the theme of the Ram for the label of 1966 recalls some of the best contemporary practitioners of the comic strip.

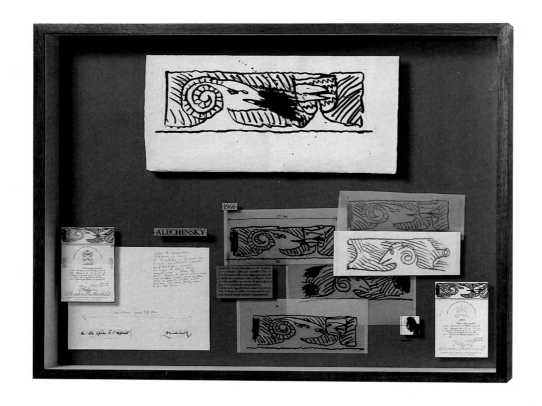

Ink
22.5 x 47.5 cm
(A second drawing, ink: ram in a bottle)

51

A native of Marseilles, César Baldaccini, known as César, was born in 1921. He studied as a classical sculptor first in Marseilles and then in Paris, where he settled in 1943. "Carrara marble was too expensive, but there was old iron lying about everywhere," he said. He has always loved scrap metal, and like some modern alchemist is able to transmute it into sculpture.

His representational period (1952–1960), during which he worked with his oxyacetylene torch to sculpt figures of both animals and human beings — *Le Poisson*, 1954; *La Grande Duchesse*, 1956 — often of fantastic appearance, came to a sudden end with the revelation that entirely changed his ideas about art: he became aware of the creative possibilities made available by modern technology and the techniques of mass production.

In 1960 this led him to exhibit for the first time his now-famous *Compressions*, initially crushed cars, then other objects compressed in the same way — bicycles, radiators — reduced under the weight of the steam hammer to the shape of the ingot they first came from.

A restless search for self-renewal made him move on, in 1966, to more malleable materials: plastic, in which he produced a gigantic cast of a thumb, then of a woman's head, then of her breast; and polyurethane, making use of its inflatability to create his much-publicized *Expansions*. These have continued to develop in size and shape, culminating in what he calls *Coulées murales* — molten murals — in 1976 and 1977.

Although firmly rooted in contemporary art and the demands of the present day — he has designed the French equivalent of the Oscar award, now known as a "César" — his work is nonetheless independent of fashion; it is always subject to change, as he is driven by his constant self-questioning and creative curiosity.

The 1967 label, in which he remains faithful to his own concern with industrial technology, clearly demonstrates the artist's independence of the conventional theme.

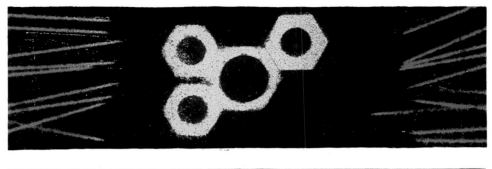

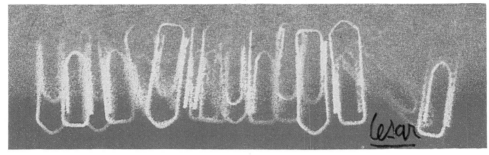

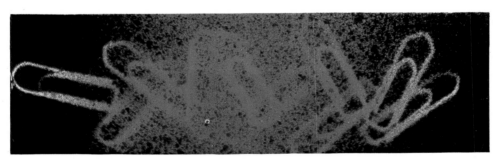

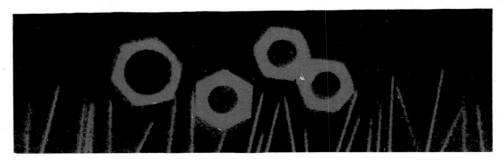

Mixed media:
five compositions
All: 3 x 11.5 cm

Born in Rome of Italian parents in 1926, Bona Tibertelli is the niece of the great painter Filippo de Pisis. After studying art in Modena, where she came under the influence of de Chirico's "Metaphysical Surrealism," she settled in Venice in 1946, working and living with her uncle, who directed and dominated her work, confirming her in her desire to be a painter.

Her marriage to André Pieyre de Mandiargues in 1950 brought her into contact with the best of the Surrealists and the intellectual avant-garde in Paris — André Breton, Francis Ponge, Jean Paulhan. In such company her talent blossomed into work of untrammeled fantasy, in which she

played with proportion and blended animate and inanimate forms in a way that was always recognizably her own: mandrake roots like giant human figures (*Le Funiculaire*, 1951), and huge seashells. Her Paris exhibition in 1952 won high praise from leading Surrealists. Her belief in Surrealism led her next to what she called "decalcomanie" (literally, children's transfers), suggesting an almost unconscious participation on the part of the artist — the automatic painting advocated and practiced by Max Ernst.

In 1958 she went to Mexico for an extended stay, her work becoming more abstract, and began to use new materials such as cement, stucco, and gravel (*Le Poème*, 1960). In this context she finally found her own individual style in collage, a technique pioneered by the Cubists. Her favorite material was cloth, which she used for *L'Homme envahissant* and also for mythological figures like Wotan and the goddess Kali.

For all its range and variety, Bona's work maintains a strong unity in its allusive but highly disciplined expression of the subconscious.

The label for 1968 is typical of her earlier style.

Gouache and gold paint
Signed at lower right
7 x 19.5 cm
(Second drawing, gouache, 7 x 19.5 cm)

A Catalan by birth, Joan Miró was born at Montroig in 1893, studied art in Barcelona, and held his first exhibition there in 1918, his painting at that time strongly affected by Van Gogh, Cézanne, and Matisse.

In Paris in 1919 he came under the influence of the aesthetic movements then in vogue, Cubism and Dadaism, before being introduced by André Masson to the Surrealists. André Breton enthusiastically welcomed him to their ranks, and went so far as to say in 1928, "Miró is probably the most Surrealist of us all."

It was in 1924 that he really found himself, producing canvases that showed a world of violent color, a world made up of vaguely alarming shapes, symbols, snakes, creatures with strange leglike extensions (*Catalan Landscape*, 1924), but with all the innocence and untrammeled imagination of children's drawings.

All Miró's work is based on this fundamental ambiguity. Are we meant to take these masks in orbit about womblike vortices as images of oedipal fixation? Or are we, first and foremost, to enjoy the exuberant energy and the humor implicit in the whirlpool of color and form that seems to mock gray, everyday reality? This strong decorative element in his work has frequently led the public to underestimate the seriousness of his intention.

Miró's inventive energy from 1927 onwards was expressed in his collages (*Danseuse espagnole*, 1928, and *Corde et personnages*, 1935); his sculptures, with their incongruous juxtapositions (*Sculpture-objet*, 1929); his sets and costumes (*Jeux d'enfants*, 1932), for the Monte Carlo Ballet; then, after the war, his frescoes, for Harvard University, and his ceramics, for Barcelona airport.

His label for Mouton Rothschild 1969 is in the mainstream of his work, always deeply original but able to adapt itself, gracefully and amusingly, as in this instance, to a specific commission. Dominated by a blood-red grape, his label also salutes the blue and yellow of the Rothschild racing colors.

Gouache
Signed at lower right
15.8 x 34 cm

Designer, engraver, painter, and sculptor, Marc Chagall was born in Vitebsk, Russia, in 1887, into an Orthodox Jewish family. He was a pupil in St. Petersburg of Léon Bakst, but was already developing his own very personal style (*Red Nude*, 1908). Working in Paris from 1910 to 1914, he met Apollinaire, Modigliani, and Soutine. He then went back to Russia, where he married Bella, a favorite model who was to become a lifelong companion.

In 1917 the Soviet government appointed him Commissar of Fine Arts in Vitebsk. There he first encouraged, and was later replaced in office by, Lissitsky and Malevitch. He went to Moscow

and from there to Paris, where he settled in 1923 and became closely involved with the Surrealists. In 1931 he illustrated La Fontaine's *Fables* and the Bible.

The rise of Nazism cast a shadow over the serene naïveté of his painting (*The White Crucifixion*, 1938), and the prevailing mood of anti-Semitism forced him in 1941 to immigrate to the United States, where Bella died in 1944.

After returning to Paris in 1947, he began working in other media: sculpture, ceramics, and stained glass (for the synagogue of the Medical Center in Jerusalem and for Metz Cathedral, 1968), and finally even fresco, accepting a commission from André Malraux to paint the ceiling of the Paris Opera (1962–1964); this was followed by two murals for the Metropolitan Opera in New York.

A synthesis of Jewish culture and the Russian tradition, Chagall's images seem to float in space, representational and symbolic at the same time; they are images of great, universally shared experiences — birth, love, and death — but seen with an innocent eye that has retained a child's love of bright colors and a fondness for the familiar farmyard animals that figure in all folk stories: the donkey and the rooster.

For the 1970 label, Chagall chose not wine itself but the living fruit of the vine, pecked by a thrush or offered by a mother to her child.

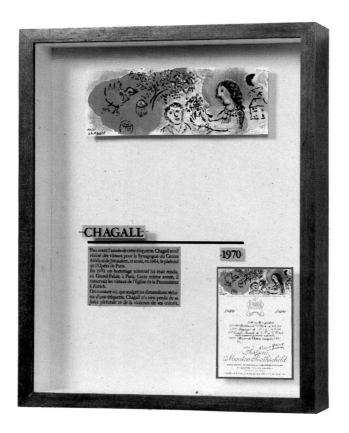

Gouache, watercolor and crayon
Signed at lower left
7.4 x 20 cm

Russian-born, then a naturalized German, and finally a Frenchman, Wassily Kandinsky (1866–1944) played a central role in the genesis and development of abstract art. Conceived originally as a radical break with the traditional *mimesis*, or imitation of reality, then as the creative *logos* in a world sometimes solid and sometimes in a state of flux, abstraction for Kandinsky is a literal sharing in the act of divine creation. "Every work of art is technically brought to birth — like the cosmos itself — through a series of catastrophes, all combining to form a symphony we call the music of the spheres. The creation of a work of art is a creation of the world," he wrote in 1913.

But this starting point was also the conclusion of a long spiritual journey: in his early days in Moscow as a lawyer and anthropologist, Kandinsky already understood, standing in front of Monet's *Haystacks*, that the impact of a work of art was not necessarily dependent on the subject represented.

His painting, on the other hand, had not yet freed itself from the style of the period, whether Impressionist or Fauvist, even though his theoretical ideas were sufficiently advanced for him to write in 1908, "I knew for certain that objective reality was limiting me as a painter, but there the ground went terrifyingly from under my feet: what was to take the place of objective reality?"

In 1910, in Munich, after a period of intense and concentrated preparation, Kandinsky produced what will always be for art historians the first abstract watercolor. The same year he painted his series of *Compositions*, justifying what he had done in a theoretical essay entitled *Concerning the Spiritual in Art*.

Although given important responsibilities by the Soviet regime after 1919, he returned to Germany in 1922 to teach at the Bauhaus, where he remained until 1932. He also pursued his theoretical work, publishing *Point and Line to Plane* in 1926, and in 1931 *Reflections on Abstract Art*.

Throughout this period, his canvases tend to combine a growing sense of geometrical discipline, daring color contrasts, and a poetic imagination that was still active and developing after his move to Paris in 1933.

The Mouton Rothschild label for 1971 shows a work from around 1930, his "architectural" period: the painting itself is now in the Louvre.

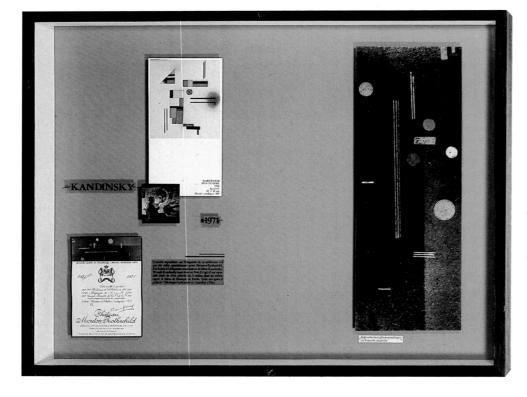

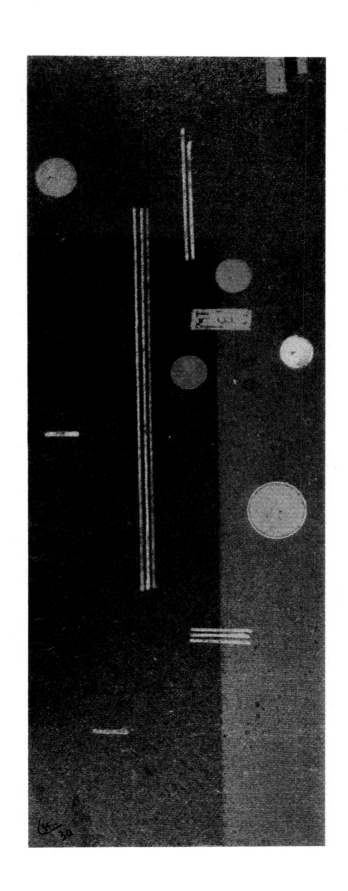

A photographic enlargement of the label; the original painting is now in the Louvre Museum

Born in Moscow, Poliakoff (1900–1969) went into exile at the time of the Revolution in 1918. After living in Turkey and several European capital cities, he finally made his home in France in 1923. He earned a living playing the guitar in Russian clubs in Paris, and studied from 1930 onwards at the Académie de la Grande Chaumière; then, from 1935 to 1937, at the Slade School in London.

On his return to Paris he joined forces first with Kandinsky and then with Robert and Sonia Delaunay, fascinated by their work on color theory. This brought him into the world of non-figurative art, where he developed a very personal style based on vivid and contrasting color.

His first abstract paintings were shown in 1945, at the Galerie de l'Esquisse, then, in 1947, at the Denise René Gallery. The same year he won the Kandinsky Prize, and he soon became known internationally, with exhibitions in Pittsburgh, Brussels, New York (1952), and at the Venice Biennale in 1962. In 1970 there was an important retrospective exhibition of his work at the Musée d'Art Moderne de la Ville de Paris.

Using a rigorous, almost architectural construction and masses of color in the form of irregular geometrical shapes, Poliakoff's painting has sometimes run the risk of becoming merely decorative. He subsequently abandoned violent contrasts for more subtle colors, orange and red, or green and blue. This gave his work a new austerity, a systematic and more deliberate abstraction.

The label for 1972 is one of his last works.

Watercolor
Signed at lower right center
24.5 x 31 cm

63

"Work as immediate and challenging as that of Picasso needs to be approached in an entirely new way: absolutely directly, honestly, without thinking, like a child. Picasso himself is forever demonstrating how it should be done, approaching everything as solid, matter-of-fact reality, treating it as *familiarly* as possible, because he immediately *understands*; he *knows*. So don't, whatever you do, put him on a pedestal like something in a mausoleum, a Great Man, when he is so obviously alive and fighting against the kind of dead definition you associate with a statue.

"Of all the crass mistakes propagated about Picasso, the most evident is the tendency to mix him up with the Surrealists, suggesting that he's rebelling against, or rather on the run from reality. Whereas in most of his paintings, the *subject* is almost always solid three dimensional *flesh and blood*, nothing to do with the misty world of the dream, and violently resisting the idea of being turned into a symbol. In other words one hundred per cent non-Surrealist. True freedom does not consist in denying reality or in escaping from it: on the contrary it means the essential recognition of reality. It is in that sense we have the right to describe Picasso as free — the *freest* painter there ever was — because he knows the precise weight of things, their scale of value, their solidity.

"Human limbs, human heads, human landscapes, human animals, human things; that is, in the end, what you find in Picasso." (Michel Leiris, *Documents*, No. 2, 1930)

"Who knows what miracle might spring out of a Picasso canvas after thirty years of silence? One day we might easily hear some rich collector say to his friends: 'You know my Picasso? This morning it started talking!'" (Jean Cocteau, *Le Rappel à l'ordre*, 1926)

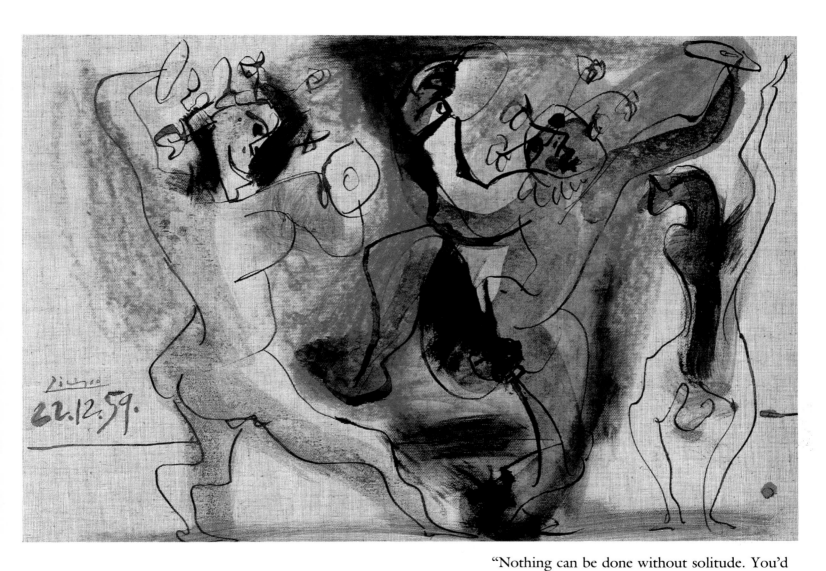

Watercolor and gouache
Signed and dated at left: 22.12.59
35 x 55 cm

"Nothing can be done without solitude. You'd never know how much I have to shut myself off. It's very hard to be on one's own nowadays because we've all got watches. Did you ever see a Saint wearing a wristwatch? I've been looking everywhere, and I can't find a single one. Not even on the ones who are supposed to be the Patron Saints of Watchmakers." (Pablo Picasso to Tériade, 1932)

The American painter Robert Motherwell was born in 1915 in Washington State. He studied philosophy, first at Stanford and then at Harvard, before training as a painter at Columbia University in New York. He has remained a philosopher who paints, or, more accurately, a painter who thinks.

After a short Surrealist period, during which he took part in the 1942 Surrealist exhibition in New York, he moved towards Abstract Expressionism, encouraged — together with Rothko and Pollock — by Peggy Guggenheim, who showed them at her gallery, Art of This Century. In 1947, the Parisian public had a chance to see his work at an exhibition at the Galerie Maeght, the first cautious appearance in France of the work of the New York School. Motherwell's work as a

painter has always gone hand in hand with his theoretical writing, and in 1948 he published a monograph on Max Ernst. Until 1952 he also edited, with the American art critic Harold Rosenberg, *Documents of Modern Art*.

His work, which was now reaching its fullest maturity, is characterized by an obsessive return to the same basic black form, massive and threatening, owing something both to the abstract and to the calligraphic traditions, and set against a background of geometrical lines and vivid color (*Elegy for the Spanish Republic*, 1954).

A typical Motherwell, the label for Mouton Rothschild 1974 shows this artist not only as a highly original talent, but also as one of the moving spirits behind the New York School.

Oil on canvas
20.5 x 61 cm

ANDY WARHOL

Born in 1930 in Philadelphia, Warhol began as a designer in an advertising agency, and first came to public attention when he won the Art Directors Club Award in 1957. He became one of the leading figures in Pop Art, exhibiting in 1962 his famous series of silk-screen prints of Coca-Cola bottles, followed by prints of Campbell's Soup cans. He later subjected Marilyn Monroe, Liz Taylor, and Jackie Kennedy to the same treatment.

This is Warhol's joke at the expense of the Consumer Society, attacking it through its most universally respected myths: manufactured articles, shown on canvas to be empty of any real content; famous faces caught and fixed in hackneyed poses that turn even them into mere objects. The artist too suffers the same symbolic but nevertheless effective destruction, becoming part of the same cardboard world of make-believe and visual deception: made-up and marketed, he himself becomes an object, a "personality"; and, as a final irony, Warhol calls his studio the "Factory," staffing it with weird creatures of the half-light, the very opposite of hardworking, clean-limbed American youth.

All Warhol's work in fact centers on a vision of death: the death of a society of automata, lulled into a dazed acceptance of consumer products, newspapers, advertising, the star system, or, more dangerous still, of cars, drugs, and even nuclear weapons.

Although he uses his familiar method of photomontage, Warhol's label for 1975 presents an affectionate image of Baron Philippe.

Mixed media
Signed with initials, lower right
Above left: 51 x 38 cm
Above right: 48.5 x 37.5 cm
Right: 49.5 x 36 cm

69

PIERRE SOULAGES

The French painter Pierre Soulages was born in the Massif Central in 1919. Absorbing the harshness of the barren countryside in which he grew up, he began by painting austere, desolate landscapes. He discovered the work of Cézanne and Picasso in the late thirties.

In 1946 his painting suddenly became more abstract: together with Hartung and Schneider, he exhibited in Paris in 1947 at the Salon des Surindependents, where he was an immediate success with the public for the originality, strength, and economy of his visual language, a language he continued to use throughout his career.

Soulages has been accorded a remarkable degree of official recognition: top awards at the São Paulo Biennale in 1953, the Tokyo International Exhibition in 1957, the Carnegie Prize in 1964, and many more. His work combines the serenity of structured, symmetrical composition and long, flowing strokes of dark color with the lyrical violence of the act of painting, evident from the kinds of instruments he has used: rakes, rubber- or leather-bladed scrapers, palette knives, spatulas, and even scrubbing brushes.

He almost always avoids color and usually paints in black. This basic monochrome is, however, sometimes varied by maroon or cobalt blue, as in the label for 1976, where Soulages has even managed to include the initials of Mouton Rothschild in the pattern of the brushstrokes.

Gouache
Signed at lower left and dated: 1976
26 x 74.5 cm

Tribute to H.M. Queen Elizabeth, the Queen Mother

At the invitation of Baron Philippe de Rothschild, the Queen Mother spent three days at Mouton on the occasion of her official visit to Bordeaux in April 1977.

To mark her stay, and with her permission, Baron Philippe dedicated that year to her as a personal tribute.

All smiles: Baron Philippe introduces the Queen Mother to Mouton's domestic staff.

TRIBUTE TO QUEEN ELIZABETH THE QUEEN MOTHER

1977

The Canadian painter Riopelle was born in Montreal in 1923, and studied there, first at the Polytechnic and later at the Academy of Fine Arts. While learning furniture design at the Ecole du Meuble he was taught and greatly influenced by the painter Paul-Emile Borduas. With him he founded the Automatisme group, advocating the use of Surrealist techniques to offer a more exciting alternative to the academicism then characteristic of Canadian painting. This challenge was backed up with a manifesto, *Refus global*, which he signed in 1948.

From 1948 to 1953 he lived in Paris, where he figured in many exhibitions with Mathieu, Hartung, and Jean-Michel Atlan. After 1954 he exhibited regularly in New York, at the Pierre Matisse gallery. He was awarded the UNESCO Prize at the Venice Biennale, and in 1967 there

was an important retrospective exhibition of his work at the Quebec museum.

Riopelle belongs to the movement known as Lyrical Abstraction. He finds his inspiration in the life force, the energy inherent in nature. His thick-textured, brilliantly colored painting suggests an initial violence, underlined by the use of a spatula or palette knife, but is nevertheless contained within the discipline of his geometrical forms (*Retourner la Marmite*, 1962).

In his most recent work (*Hiboux*, 1970; *Ficelles et autres jeux*, 1976), he has moved closer to nature, and to the celebration of local traditions, in the costume and customs of northern Canada.

For the 1978 label, Riopelle submitted two schemes: it proved impossible to choose between them, so they were both used, each one for half the vintage.

Ink and oil
Diameter: 19 cm
(Four other designs in ink are shown in the case opposite)

75

Born in 1928, in Kyoto, into a family of artists, Hisao Domoto is the nephew of Insho Domoto, a painter much loved in his native Japan. Initially he studied classical Japanese painting before traveling to Europe for the first time in 1952, where he gained the experience of Western art which led him to an eventual break with his traditional training.

In 1955 he returned to Paris to enroll in the Ecole des Beaux-Arts, and he also attended the Atelier de la Grande Chaumière. He had his first exhibition in Paris at the Galerie Stadler. The success of this exhibition took him to New York in 1959 for a show at the Martha Jackson Gallery. In 1960 he returned to Japan. His work now became more personal, with the superposition of bands of strongly contrasting colors in geometrical compositions. For this he won the Arthur Ligwa Prize at the Venice Biennale in 1964.

Towards the end of the sixties his work developed in a new direction, which he was to call "Possibilities of Chain Reaction." He took as his dominant theme the circle, about which he writes: "The circle is the purest of all forms and lends itself to a common means of expression that allows a dialogue between nations; it is also a symbolic form." This theme of the circle finds its natural extension in the chain, both sharing the same sense of momentum, emphasized by the play of radiating and contrasting colors (*Sun Ring*, 1975; *Chain Reaction Number One*, 1977; *Lunar Eclipse*, 1977).

The Mouton label belongs to this light and decorative period, seen in Europe at an exhibition of his work at the Musée d'Art Moderne de la Ville de Paris in 1979. This label is the first commission given to an artist from the Far East.

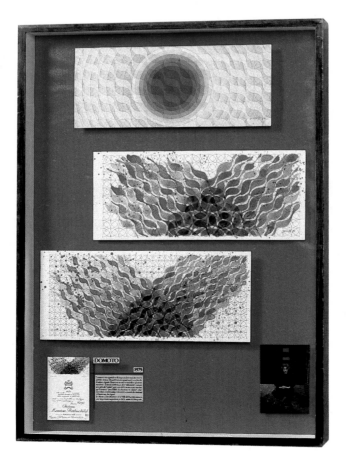

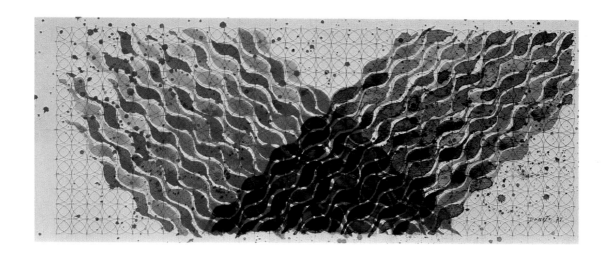

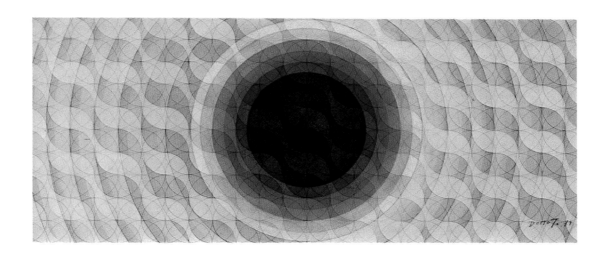

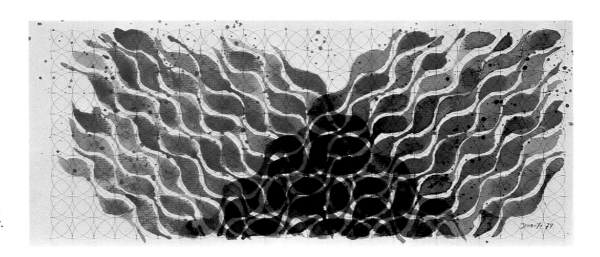

Ink and acrylic
25.5 x 54.5 cm
(Two other paintings:
the first ink and gouache,
the second ink and acrylic.
All signed at lower right)

77

The pioneer of Lyrical Abstraction, Hans Hartung was born in Leipzig in 1904, and completed a solid grounding in philosophy and the history of art at the university while working on drawings and watercolors of an abstract tendency. His formative years in Dresden, Leipzig, and Munich were important for the conflicting influences of Kandinsky and of the Expressionists Nolde and Kokoschka.

After a first exhibition in Dresden in 1931 and periods of living in France and Mallorca, he decided to leave Nazi Germany and settled permanently in Paris in 1935. He joined the Foreign Legion in 1939, was seriously wounded and lost a leg. Having become a naturalized Frenchman, he began painting again in 1945, and held his first exhibition in Paris in 1947 at the Lydia Conti Gallery.

Hartung has also worked as an engraver and lithographer. He won the Grand Prix at the Venice Biennale in 1960, and has been a member of the French Academy of Fine Arts since 1977.

His love of what he called "acting on canvas" is an attitude towards painting that had now ripened into a conviction. Rejecting geometrical abstraction as too dogmatic, he offers instead a kind of painting based on spontaneity and the physical act of putting the paint on the canvas, involving all the violence of human gesture, and through that, of the painter's inner self.

The label for 1980 is typical of his work: using a plain-colored ground, he paints in long sweeping black strokes that seem to claw across the canvas, expressing a sense of rebellious liberty reminiscent of American Action Painting but still contained within the disciplines of calligraphy.

Acrylic on wood
4.2 x 10 cm
(Three other paintings, all acrylic on wood)

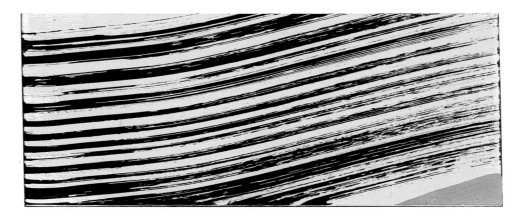

Born in Nice in 1928, Arman Fernandez, known as Arman, studied there before going to the Ecole du Louvre in Paris. Influenced by the pictorial experiments of his friend Yves Klein, he joined him and other painters, together with the art critic Pierre Restany, to form the *Nouveaux Réalistes* group in 1960. This move came as a reaction to the then dominant abstract tendency in painting. Arman himself celebrates familiar objects, from revolvers to coffeepots, in crazy assemblages conveying a sense of their solid reality.

After his "cachets," or seals, of 1956, printed directly onto the canvas, Arman attempted various approaches to the representation of objective reality, by mounting techniques, even by destroying the object in question. After the controversial exhibition *Les Poubelles* (Dustbins) in 1960 came the fixing of industrial scrap in blocks of transparent Plexiglas—*Accumulations Renault* (1969)—and finally the notorious *Colères*, the violent dismembering of artifacts, notably musical instruments, violins, and pianos. At times, too, Arman shaped the aspirations of American Pop Art, in a desire to alienate a consumer society from its own consumer products.

Since 1955, Arman has come to prominence through dozens of one-man exhibitions all over the world, and has won many international awards.

The 1981 label returns to a theme used earlier by the Cubists, that of the violin, but treated in a typically Arman style, catching random echoes of its fragmented form.

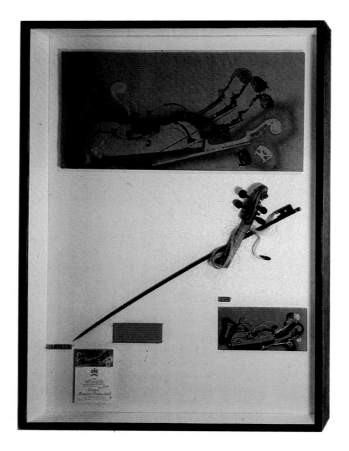

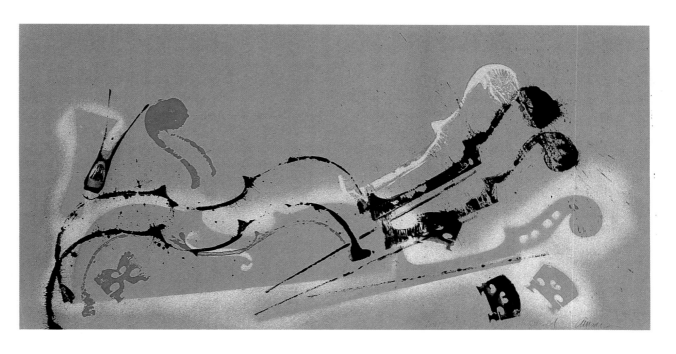

Ink, gouache, gold paint
Signed at lower right and annotated:
"Projet n° 15 Mouton-Rothschild"
32.5 x 65 cm
(Two other paintings, also ink, gouache, gold paint)

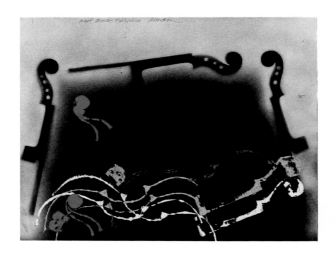
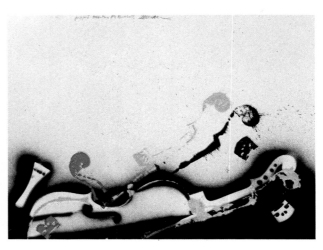

Part Two

THE HOUSE

· ·

The Story of Mouton Rothschild

In the early years of the eighteenth century the Médoc was largely in the hands of the old feudal landlords, consisting of a few great estates given over to mixed farming, with wine only a part of the annual produce. Nicolas-Alexandre, Marquis de Ségur, lived at Château Lafite as lord of all Pauillac, including the present estate of Mouton and even Château Latour.

The wine at this time was, for the most part, drunk as soon as it was in the barrel, the process of aging still yielding very inconsistent results. It was nonetheless already being shipped abroad, to St. James's Palace in London, as well as to the French Court at Versailles.

By 1740, the Médoc had begun to be broken up into smaller estates devoted exclusively to growing wine. The land belonging to the Marquis de Ségur was also either sold off or divided by inheritance into more manageable units, like Château Mouton d'Armailhacq and Château Brane-Mouton. The word *Mouton* is derived from *Mothon*, which comes in turn from *motte*, a mount or hillock; *Brane* was the name of the owners of the newly independent estate, the Barons de Brane.

1853. On May 11, 1853, Baron Nathaniel de Rothschild, of the English branch of the famous banking family, bought Château Brane-Mouton, comprising eighty-six acres of vines in the parish of Pauillac, for 1,125,000 gold francs. He renamed it Château Mouton Rothschild.

At that time it was a château in no more than name. Its only buildings were stables and a few sheds around the farmyard. Isolated and inhospitable, it was not a place its new owner would ever want to go to, let alone visit for any length of time. What Baron Nathaniel's new acquisition did provide, though, was a fine wine that he could give his more distinguished guests, and moreover a wine with his name on it.

1855. Seeking to impose some order on its display at the Exposition Universelle of 1855, the Bordeaux Chamber of Commerce carried out an official classification of all the wine grown in that part of France, the so-called *Classement de 1855*. Mouton Rothschild, given the quality of its wine, seemed a natural candidate for the highest rating, the title of *Premier Cru*, or first growth. But several things were against the award of this accolade — the change of ownership only two years earlier; the English nationality of the new owner; and the dilapidated condition of the

Charlotte, Baroness Nathaniel de Rothschild (1825–1899), by Ary Scheffer

Baron Nathaniel de Rothschild (1812–1870)

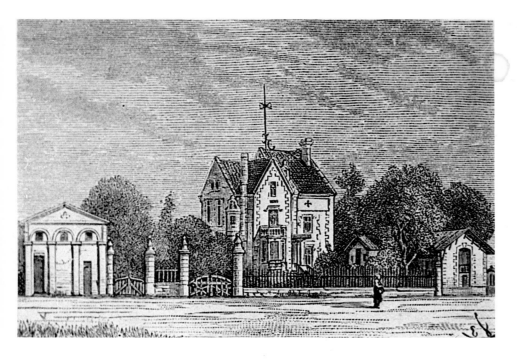

View of Petit Mouton *in 1893. On the left, the south end of the farm building that will eventually become* Grand Mouton

Bullock teams returning from plowing, at the end of the nineteenth century

Baron James de Rothschild (1844–1881)

Thérèse, Baroness James de Rothschild (1847–1931)

estate. The wine was classified a *Second Cru* but, as a consolation prize, given the title of *Premier des Seconds*.

1870. Baron Nathaniel died. His son Baron James, a Frenchman by birth, inherited Mouton Rothschild. A few years later, he made the decision to build a house there, alongside the old farm buildings, where he could stay. He died in 1881, before it was completed.

1882. Thérèse, Baron James's widow and grandmother of the present owner, finished the house; a gabled villa with pointed turrets and a colored glass veranda in the style of the period. Mouton Rothschild finally had its château. Ironically, this house is now known as *Petit Mouton* (Little Mouton).

1883–1922. During the years that followed, there were very occasional visits of a few days at a time by the Baroness James, who was to survive her husband by fifty years. She was the first member of the family ever to travel regularly to the Médoc, despite the slow train journey and the long drive in a horse and cart over forty-five miles of rutted roads from the station at Bordeaux.

Accommodation was still spartan in the extreme. The Baroness spent her time visiting the sick and doing other good works, but did not concern herself with the problems of running the estate, which was left in the hands of a succession of managers. Her son, Baron Henri, a doctor and dramatist, who had been born in 1872, took no interest in the property, which was then a very small part of the family possessions.

Henri's son Philippe, on the other hand, born in 1902 and sent to school in Bordeaux in 1916, frequently spent long periods of time there and fell in love with it — the people, the countryside, the secret world of wine.

1922. On October 22, 1922, Baron Henri officially handed over the running of Mouton Rothschild to his son. Everything was still very much as it had been in the nineteenth century; although the estate was without running water, electricity, or proper roads, Philippe went to work with a will, convinced that his future lay in wine and in realizing the huge potential he was sure the place possessed. He set about renovating the estate and introducing more advanced techniques.

The managers, maîtres de chai, *and* maîtres vignerons *at Mouton Rothschild about* 1900

Mathilde, Baroness Henri de Rothschild (1874–1926), by François Flamingue

Baron Henri de Rothschild (1872–1947) by Trice

Elisabeth, Baroness Philippe de Rothschild (1902–1945), by Christian Bérard

Baron Philippe de Rothschild (born 1902)

Pauline, Baroness Philippe de Rothschild (1908–1976); photograph by Cecil Beaton

*The wedding of Philippine de Rothschild to actor Jacques Sereys, in 1961;
the couple is seen here surrounded by Rothschilds*

*Camille, Philippe, and Julien Sereys de Rothschild,
by Paddie in 1975*

89

The estate workers at
Mouton in the twenties

The Cuvier in the twenties,
with the new wine being
transferred from the vats
into the barrels

The vat-men at Mouton Rothschild at harvest time during the early years of the century

Baron Philippe in 1922, at the age of twenty   *An estate worker, Marie Charbotel, about 1930*

Baron Philippe in the wine press, watching the grapes being separated from the stalks; about 1930

1924. A revolutionary step: the entire harvest at Mouton Rothschild was bottled at the château. This brave new departure had immense repercussions, because a direct relationship was established between producer and consumer, creating a new sense of confidence in the product. The importance of this new procedure was very soon recognized, and the *Premiers Crus* — Lafite, Latour, Haut-Brion, and Margaux — followed suit, bottling their own wine. Shortly afterwards, at Baron Philippe's suggestion, they joined him to form the *Association des Premier Crus*. In 1929, Château d'Yquem, the best of the Sauternes, also joined the group. By working together as a team, the Association des Premiers Crus became a potent force in the wine market.

1924–1927. Bottling at the château meant that more space was needed, wine requiring between two and three years in the barrel before it is bottled. This meant a new building, designed to the Baron's specifications by the Parisian architect Charles Siclis. No expense was spared on building materials and craftsmanship; new techniques of lighting were introduced, and the design has a simplicity of line that still takes the breath away. This was to be the *Grand Chai* — the word *chai* being related to the English "shed," the Great Storehouse — and the highlight for visitors to Mouton.

1927–1933. The harvest for 1927 was not up to the standards of quality required to carry the name of Mouton Rothschild. It was sold, unsuccessfully, under the trademark *Carruades de Mouton Rothschild*.

   In the two years that followed, the problem of quality did not arise, 1928 and 1929 being among the greatest vintages of the century.

The Association des Premiers Crus, *also known as the* Groupe des Six, *about 1930. Left to right: André Gibert, Baron Philippe de Rothschild, Comte René de Beaumont, Pierre Moreau, Baron Robert de Rothschild, Comte Bertrand de Lur-Saluces, representing, respectively, Château Haut-Brion, Château Mouton Rothschild, Château Latour, Château Margaux, Château Lafite-Rothschild, Château d'Yquem*

The back of the Grand Chai *about 1930: horses were still
in use to move the barrels. Carlu's design for the 1924 label
is painted on the wall*

The Grand Chai, *built in 1926, here in photograph of 1980
by Michel Géney.*

*Philippine, Baron Philippe's daughter, at the age of one,
flanked by two imperials of Mouton Rothschild*

The summers of 1930, 1931, and 1932 were all bad, with the result that, once again, the wine was not good enough to be sold as Château Mouton Rothschild. Baron Philippe and his managers had to find an answer. They came up with a name that immediately won unanimous approval: *Mouton Cadet*. In French *cadet* means the youngest son, and Philippe was the youngest of three children. All the wine made on the estate for those three years, but only for those years, was sold under the Mouton Cadet label. The name was an instant success.

1933. This year saw two significant developments: first, Baron Philippe bought Château Mouton d'Armailhacq from the Comte de Ferrand. This estate had been classified as a Fifth Growth in 1855, with ninety-nine acres of good vines, and a leafy park. The outbuildings at Mouton d'Armailhacq could now accommodate the machinery and agricultural equipment that had previously cluttered up the area around the house at Mouton Rothschild.

Second, he bought the *Société Vinicole de Pauillac*, a small wine company in the town of Pauillac with premises in an advanced state of disrepair.

1934–1939. In the immediate prewar years, Mouton continued to move into the twentieth century, now at increasing speed: electricity was installed, roads built, even the telephone was connected. An elegant *Salle des Banquets* was built beside the *Grand Chai*, with more than enough space for local dinners and for entertaining distinguished visitors.

*Baron Philippe and Philippine,
at Mouton in 1948*

Château Mouton d'Armailhacq: the owner's house, built
in the mid-nineteenth century

Petit Mouton, *built 1884*

Promotional material of the early thirties for Mouton
d'Armailhacq, then the property of the Comte de Ferrand

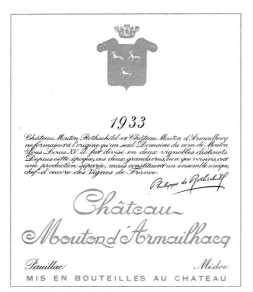

1933

*Label for Château Mouton d'Armailhacq
1933; the year of purchase,
a château joins the fold*

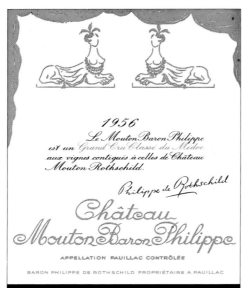

1956

1956: Mouton d'Armailhacq *becomes*
Mouton Baron Philippe*:*
*promotion to full status as a Baron
Philippe wine*

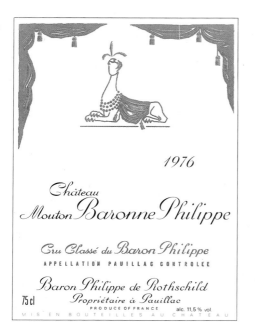

1976

1979

At the same time, the Société Vinicole de Pauillac also began to market *Mouton Cadet*, from then on a trademark entirely independent of Château Mouton Rothschild. Mouton Cadet would in future carry the designation "Appellation Bordeaux" on the label, meaning that Mouton Cadet wine could come from a wider area, but only within the strictly defined limits of the Bordeaux region.

1940–1944. The war. The estate was first requisitioned by the Vichy Government, then occupied by the Germans, who turned the house into a military headquarters and built barracks for the troops. An officer, known locally as the *Weinführer* and personally appointed by Goering, supervised the business side, ensuring the continuity of wine production throughout the war years. The house itself, however, suffered considerably.

1945. With the Liberation, Baron Philippe returned from fighting with the Allied Forces to find his daughter Philippine miraculously still safe. His wife, the first Baroness Philippe, Philippine's mother, had been deported to a concentration camp at Ravensbrück, and had never returned. Philippe and Philippine came back to find Mouton badly damaged, but still standing. The former German lords of the manor, now prisoners of war, were employed to demolish the military installations and to build the long straight drive that runs through the park of Mouton d'Armailhacq; today, laid with white

1976: Mouton Baron Philippe *becomes* Mouton Baronne Philippe *in memory of the Baroness Pauline*

1979: The most recent label for Château Mouton Baronne Philippe

gravel, this drive contributes greatly to the elegance of the approach to Mouton. This year also marked the beginning of the regular use of illustrated labels.

1947. Death of Baron Henri de Rothschild. In the settlement of the inheritance, Baron Philippe bought back his brother's and sister's shares in the property.

1948–1954. Throughout the postwar years the momentum continued to increase. Baron Philippe, at last sole master of Mouton, settled down to complete his life's work — a work of love, indeed, a work of art. As well as restoring all parts of the estate to full production and expanding the operation in Pauillac, he set about restoring the house, undertaking major works of improvement and decoration.

1954. This year saw Baron Philippe's marriage to Pauline Fairfax-Potter, an American by birth who had lived in Europe for some years and who had been his constant companion since 1951. She now became the second Baroness Philippe de Rothschild. With the application of her creative energy and talent, Mouton was transfigured, benefiting as much from her taste and sense of style as it did from her charm and her talent as a hostess.

1956. To end the frequent confusion between Armailhacq and the brandy Armagnac, and more important, to make this excellent wine a full member of the family, *Château Mouton d'Armailhacq* became *Château Mouton Baron Philippe*.

Baron Philippe and friend, in the Long Room, *1982*

The Baron and the Baroness in the Long Room *at Mouton in 1962; photograph by Cecil Beaton*

Grand Mouton: *the* Library

Venetian glass and Dutch glass-holder,
both seventeenth century. Height: 24 cm

Dancing satyr in bronze, with a wineskin and a whip.
Hellenistic, third to second century B.C. Height: 24.5 cm

The Salle des Negociants, *the merchants' room, where*
the official visit to Mouton begins

1957–1961. After their marriage, Baron Philippe and his wife worked together as a team to make constant improvements to Mouton. What had formerly been a hayloft above old machinery sheds, and lumber-rooms on the west side of the courtyard surrounding *Petit Mouton*, now became *La Bibliothèque*, a library of very original design, and *La Grande Pièce*, a long drawing room looking out through the semi-circular windows of the old hayloft over an unbroken sea of vines. They also made bedrooms for themselves and their private guests.

The whole building now became known as *Grand Mouton*.

1961. On March 4, at Mouton, Baron Philippe's only child, Philippine, then a young actress at the Comédie Française, married Jacques Sereys, a senior member of the same company. They were to have three children: a daughter, Camille, born in 1961; a son Philippe, born in 1963; and a second son, Julien, born in 1971.

1962. The completion of a plan that had been maturing for many years: a private museum opened by André Malraux, then French minister of culture. Housed at the very center of Mouton, in one of its oldest buildings, like the treasury of a monastery sited between the monks' cells and the cloister, it brought together masterpieces of all periods and many different civilizations, all works inspired by wine. This private museum represented the culmination of years of patient and passionate involvement by the Baron and the Baroness, and travels that had taken them half-way around the world, as far as Japan and the Soviet Union.

The Salle des Banquets, *the banqueting hall at* Grand Mouton, *also disrespectfully known as the "toboggan room" for its oddly angled ceiling*

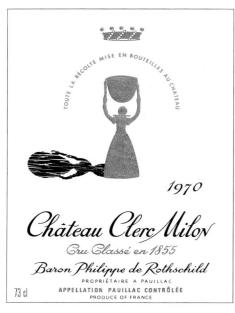

Above: The label of Château Clerc Milon based on the Jungfraubecher *in the Mouton Museum*

Above right: A marriage cup in silver-gilt and silver, of German workmanship and dated 1609, known as a Jungfraubecher. These cups were traditionally made for the marriage ceremony: the husband drank from the larger cup formed by the skirt, and the wife from the smaller bowl above. The words along the hem of the dress read "He that drinks herefrom, either beer or wine, shall ever hold me in most high esteem." Height: 31 cm

Right: Pear-wood statuette of a grape-picker. The base, and the top and bottom of the hod, are in silver gilt. The feather in the figure's hat and the handle of his stick are gold. German, from Bavaria, end of sixteenth century. Height: 33 cm

The Mouton Museum and the regular tours of the *chais* and the cellars, conducted with poetic charm by the *Maître de Chai*, Raoul Blondin, increasingly put Mouton on the map, and drew thousands of visitors every year.

1970. Baron Philippe bought Château Clerc-Milon, *Cru Classé* in 1855 and an estate much in need of renovation. Thanks to the skill of the team at Mouton, the quality of this wine has rapidly improved and today fully deserves its status as a *Cru Baron Philippe.*

1973. A year to remember: Château Mouton Rothschild was legally recognized as a *Premier Cru*. Despite the 1855 classification as *Second Cru*, Mouton had always been considered equal to any of the *Premiers Crus* and sold for many years at the same price. Baron Philippe, finding this discrepancy between the legal position and the actual state of affairs intolerable, began a campaign in 1953 to have the classification changed.

Few causes have been fought with more tenacity, not only against bureaucratic red tape and the dead weight of the system, but also against the reluctance of certain *Grands Crus* to change an arrangement that was clearly to their advantage.

Nevertheless, with the support of other growers and of prominent personalities in Bordeaux, Baron Philippe was eventually victorious. On June 21, 1973, Jacques Chirac, then minister of agriculture, signed the proclamation that officially made Mouton equal to the other *Premiers Crus*. Newspapers all over the world carried the news, and loyal fans of Mouton celebrated its well-deserved triumph.

Until then, the motto on Mouton's coat of arms had been *Premier ne puis, Second ne daigne, Mouton suis* ("First I cannot be, Second I disdain,

Mouton I am"), inspired by that of the Ducs de Rohan: "King I cannot be, Prince I disdain, Rohan I am." The old motto now had to be modified: *Premier je suis, Second je fus, Mouton ne change* ("First I am, Second I was, I Mouton do not change"). This historic vintage bears the label with Picasso's watercolor.

1976. Baroness Philippe de Rothschild died in California. In homage to her work, the name of Château Mouton Baron Philippe was changed to Château Mouton Baronne Philippe.

1977. Queen Elizabeth, the Queen Mother, on an official visit to the Médoc, spent three days at Mouton. Her lasting popularity in France, dating from the dark years of the war, won her an enthusiastic reception from local people in Pauillac and the surrounding villages.

1979. The growing number of tourists converging on Mouton, individually and in groups, made it imperative to improve facilities for receiving them. This led to the construction in the park of a new building, *Le Club*: a reception room where visitors could be told something of what they were about to see before the visit began. Harmonizing perfectly with the white stone of the older buildings, but of strikingly modern design and carrying on one exterior wall Kenneth Armitage's monumental sculpture *The Sun*, it completes a whole new phase of building begun and supervised by Baron Philippe; with curving stone walls, low tiled roofs, and clean geometrical lines, it is a continuation of the Mouton style.

Above: The Club, *built to receive a growing number of visitors. On the wall,* The Sun, *by English sculptor Kenneth Armitage (1960)*

Philippine de Rothschild and her father, by the Lion Fountain at Mouton

Recently completed stone-walled buildings seen from the windows at Grand Mouton. They are used for garaging cars, which are concealed from view by the walls of circular plan, with half-roofs of shallow tiles.

1981. In February Madame Philippine de Rothschild made her first official visit to the United States, to Los Angeles, New York, and Miami; at banquets, press conferences, on radio and in television interviews, she carried on her father's work with characteristic energy.

In June, Baron Philippe published in France *Vivre la Vigne*, the history of the dynasty, but above all relating the adventure of Mouton, told by the man who has devoted his life to it.

In September, Philippine de Rothschild, establishing herself in the role of Mouton's roving ambassador, opened the first exhibition of original paintings for the Mouton labels in Montreal. The success of the exhibition confirmed the extraordinary prestige attaching to this *Premier Cru*.

1982. Japan Year: In June and July, the exhibition toured Japan, sponsored by the SEIBU Group, in honor of the painter Hisao Domoto, who designed the 1979 label.

1983–84. . . . The exhibition marches on, carrying the Mouton style from Tokyo to Edinburgh, from London to the New World.

Philippine de Rothschild with her father, Baron Philippe, in the Long Room *(1981); photograph by Norman Parkinson*

Hanging the exhibition in Japan

The Mouton Museum

THE CONCEPT OF THE MUSEUM

Wine museums in general are not concerned with things of beauty. They are intended to preserve the various tools and implements used in the cultivation of the vine and in wine making at different periods of history and in different parts of the world. They appeal, in the main, to agricultural historians and the occasional member of the public with nothing better to do on a wet afternoon.

The museum at Mouton, on the other hand, aims at something entirely different: it too, has on display objects relating to wine and the vine, but they are without exception works of art in their own right, in many cases worthy of inclusion in any of the great national collections.

Art lovers will find a wealth of exhibits from very different cultures, from the dawn of civilization to the present day, and of an amazing variety, both in material and in form: gold and silver work, pictures, tapestries, porcelains, ceramics, bronzes, ivories, glass, and sculptures.

The original core of the museum consisted of the work of German gold- and silversmiths from the fourteenth to the seventeenth centuries, originally the property of Baron Carl von Rothschild. This already constituted a remarkable collection of drinking vessels and jugs, cups, ewers, and chalices.

From this beginning, Baron Philippe and his wife Baroness Pauline decided to create a museum of Wine in Art, the Mouton Museum. In 1962, it was opened to the general public.

In the Mouton Museum

BUILDING THE MUSEUM

The museum covers in all an area of 2300 square feet. The ground plan and organization of the exhibits were worked out by the Baron and Baroness themselves in collaboration with the Bordeaux architect André Conte. The stonework, tiling, electrical wiring, carpentry, the installation of the carpets and all fixtures and fittings were carried out by workers on the estate and local craftsmen from Pauillac.

The *Salle principale*, the main room, was originally a storehouse for barrels and has retained its original shape: visitors enter the room down two gently sloping ramps once used for rolling in the barrels. This is the largest room, occupying a space of 976 square feet, and opens out into six smaller rooms, each of which in the old days had its own particular use.

The display cases are of varying size, some let into the thickness of the wall, some freestanding on light metal pillars and asymmetrically arranged in the different rooms. The same attention to design is evident in the internal arrangement of the cases, each one lined in raw silk, in a sequence of subtly harmonizing colors, with the objects displayed on silk-covered stands of varying height to make the fullest use of the available space. Every work of art is independently lit, the spotlights often creating surprising effects.

The floor, too, with rose-pink ceramic tiles punctuated by black roundels, with the checkered effect of grey slate and turquoise blue tiles, contrasts with what remains of the original paving.

View of the Salle principale

View of the Rinçoir

Above: Albrecht Dürer's famous engraving, made in 1501, showing Nemesis, or Destiny, reins in her left hand to curb the wicked, and a wine cup in her right to reward the good.
40 x 30 cm

Above, right: Pear-shaped covered drinking cup in silver-gilt made about 1650 by a master silversmith of Augsburg, based on the cup in Dürer's engraving of Nemesis. Height: 38 cm

Right: Embossed silver jug, engraved and partially gilded, made in Augsburg, bearing the Gelb family mark, and probably the work of Melchior Gelb (1617–1654). Height: 32 cm

A BRIEF TOUR

The works of art are not arranged as might be expected, in strict chronological order. Most are grouped according to the materials from which they are made or according to similarities of style, which produces some striking juxtapositions. Other works have been singled out, intentionally isolated to emphasize some particular aspect of their workmanship.

The Salle principale. The main room is devoted primarily to the Carl von Rothschild Collection, consisting of gold and silver work, some pieces of antique ivory and tapestries of different periods.

Among the gold and silver works, many of them made by the smiths of Nuremberg and Augsburg, the following may be of greatest interest:

A silver-gilt covered cup, made about 1650 and based on an engraving by Albrecht Dürer of 1501; a fifteenth-century silver-gilt ewer of Flemish origin, in hexagonal form, a rare survival of the gold and silverwork vessels in use at the court of the Dukes of Burgundy; a marriage cup, called a *Jungfraubecher*, of 1609, familiar to wine-lovers as the emblem of Château Clerc-Milon.

Among the ivories, the most remarkable work is unquestionably a chalice decorated with figures in relief and carved in 1710 in Dusseldorf by Antonio Leoni.

The tapestries include in particular a rare set of five showing the stages of wine making, and one from the Elizabethan period representing Tarquin and Lucretia and showing the face of Queen Elizabeth herself.

A very rare tapestry, woven between 1480 and 1530, probably somewhere near Strasburg, showing the grape harvest and the use of the comporte, *a sort of tub carried by two men. This tapestry is the fourth in a series of five, each illustrating the various stages of wine making at the period. Height: 2.72 m; Width: 2.62 m.*

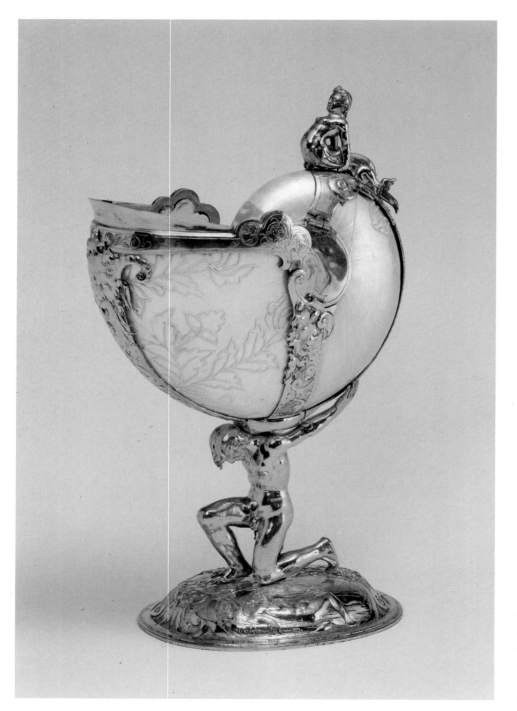

A silver-gilt dish, inspired by an engraving by Abraham Bosse dated 1635, made in Augsburg by the master silver-smith Melchior Gelb in 1654, the year of his death. The rim of the dish is ornamented with a design of baroque scrolls linked by six lion heads. Diameter: 27 cm

Left: Nautilus-form cup, made of a seashell placed on the shoulders of a kneeling figure in the traditional posture of Atlas supporting the globe. Mounted in silver-gilt on an upturned shield. German, probably from Nuremberg. End of the sixteenth century. Height: 25 cm

Right: Two Commedia dell'Arte figures, Pulcinella and Pantalone, in gold, pearls, enamel, and precious stones, attributed to the goldsmith Dinglinger (1664–1731). This extraordinarily delicate piece was a present from Count Orloff to the Empress Catherine the Great of Russia. Height: 11 cm

The Salle italienne. The Italian room, which covers an area of 240 square feet, contains paintings that include *The Infant Bacchus* by Guido Reni (1575–1642), furniture made between 1750 and 1760 that belonged to the last Doge of Genoa, and embroidery of the same period.

The Salle du Trésor. The Treasury, 120 square feet in area, contains smaller exhibits remarkable for their precious materials—for example, a white-wine pourer of green jade, with a ram's head, encrusted with gold and rubies, once the property of the Mogul princes; also two Commedia dell'Arte figures and a pair of owls of rare Swiss workmanship.

The Salle des Tableaux. This room, covering an area of 65 square feet, contains a collection of paintings, with seventeenth-century Dutch still lifes hanging next to modern works by Rouault, Juan Gris, and Giacometti, and also the *Bacchanale* by Picasso, which illustrates the label for Mouton Rothschild 1973.

Pencil drawing (1910) by Juan Gris, of a young man (probably Pablo Picasso) in a Parisian café, being solicited by an older woman. 35 x 28 cm

The Rinçoir. The Scullery, seven hundred square feet, contains porcelain and glass. Among the porcelains are a Chinese wine jug with a floral design of the K'ang Hsi period; several pieces of "blue and white" porcelain, including a rare flask of the Ming Dynasty mounted in silver gilt by European craftsmen; examples of Dutch, French, and English biscuit-work of the seventeenth and eighteenth centuries, and valuable Persian ceramics from the ninth to the fourteenth centuries. There is also an important collection of Venetian glasses in various styles, miraculously still intact after two hundred or three hundred years, and larger Dutch and German wrought goblets of the seventeenth century.

Wine flask in the form of a grotesque figure sitting astride a barrel. His plume serves as a stopper. Delft pottery, dated 1756. Height: 41 cm

Two covered drinking cups in the shape of owls, in boxwood and silver-gilt. The tops of the heads lift off and form the lids. These owls belonged to the Empress Catherine the Great of Russia. Swiss, sixteenth century, dated 1561. Height: 29 cm

Ceramic plaque showing cellarmen tasting wine in the barrel. Delft work, end of seventeenth century. 23 x 25 cm

Three Chinese pieces (left to right): A tall wine jug in porcelain, with a closed container in the base for boiling water to keep the wine hot. Green period of the K'ang Hsi dynasty (1662–1723). Height: 40 cm; Diameter: 13 cm. A pair of enamel candlesticks from Canton, eighteenth century. Height: 15.5 cm. Enamel Canton jug decorated with rustic scenes, eighteenth century. Height: 23 cm; Diameter: 14 cm

Pair of shoes used as drinking vessels, polychrome. Delft pottery. End of seventeenth century.

Pair of ewers in the Persian style, Peking enamel, polychrome. Chinese, nineteenth century. Height: 42 cm A gift to Baron Philippe on his eightieth birthday

Silver, silver-gilt, and gold dish showing King Bahram V and his concubine mounted on a camel. According to legend, she challenged him to turn a male deer into a female and back again. He tears out the antlers of a stag, thus making it a "doe" (left). Then, with unerring aim, he plants two arrows between its ears, turning it back into a stag (right). Sassanian period, fifth century A.D. Diameter: 22 cm

The Salle des Sassanides. The Sassanian room, 195 square feet, includes a remarkable collection of works of art from Persia—goblets, saucers, jugs—from the period of Amlach art (ninth to eighth centuries B.C.) to the Sassanian period (third to seventh centuries A.D.).

This room also contains Egyptian pieces, including a bas-relief in stone from Sakkara (Fifth Dynasty), Greek pottery and marbles, as well as several Roman mosaics. From the Scullery, a staircase with Lippold's dazzling metal sculpture *The Spirit of the Vine*, leads down to the small Pre-Columbian Room, where there are several statuettes in terracotta found in tombs in Mexico and Peru.

This necessarily very brief synopsis hardly covers half the wonders visitors will discover for themselves. This is a collection which is still growing, sometimes to the surprise even of its owner. The latest acquisition is a pair of superb Chinese wine ewers, a present to Baron Philippe from his family and friends on the occasion of his eightieth birthday—a small tribute paid to the founders who began this remarkable venture that now allows a wide public to understand that great art can have its roots in a humble vineyard.

Left: Pottery figure of a hunchback drinking from a bowl. In his right hand what appears to be a rattle, suggesting a musician. Mexican, from the state of Colima, first to fifth century A.D. A gift from John Huston to Baron Philippe. Height: 30 cm

Right: Bas-relief of young woman with a tiger-skin fixed at the shoulder with a clasp; she is possibly offering wine. Egypt eighteenth dynasty, 1550 B.C. Height: 38 cm

Part Three

THE WINES

. . . .

The Cuvier, *as the visitor sees it today. Through the door,*
the Infant Bacchus holding the head of Silenus

The Wine behind the Label

1945

One of the greatest of all vintages.
Mouton '45: A Churchill of a wine. It still has a magnificent, deep, almost opaque appearance, ruby with a pronounced mahogany rim. Highly concentrated, intense blackcurrant Cabernet-Sauvignon aroma, touch of cinnamon—and flavour to match. Drink now–2050.

1946

An odd vintage, which suffered from an unusual invasion of locusts.
Mouton '46: A calm, deep, rich bouquet—no edginess of overmaturity or decay; dry, pronounced Cabernet-Sauvignon flavour. Still excellent, but becoming slightly lean, with a touch of stalky greenness. Drink up.

1947

Another postwar milestone. . . . big, warm, fleshy, generous wines.
Mouton '47: An opulent wine; very deep, brick-red colour; magnificent, gingery Mouton-Cabernet nose; great rich flavour, perfect balance and condition, exquisite aftertaste. Consistent since early 1960s. Drink now–1990.

1948

A rough diamond, a character, but lacking polish and charm.
Mouton '48: Deeper than the '47; rich, forthcoming bouquet, reminiscent of the '45 with cinnamonlike overtones. A dry wine. Slightly bitter finish. Massive. Drink now–1995.

1949

A great vintage. Fine, supple, beautifully balanced wines.

Mouton '49: A great wine. Medium colour, fine, mature; fabulous flowery bouquet, a sort of quintessence of Cabernet-Sauvignon; medium dry, medium body now, very flavoury, combining great delicacy with richness. Perfect now, will keep though gently fading.

1950

Abundant vintage, of uneven quality.
Mouton '50: Deep coloured, lovely bouquet, flavoury and quite a lot of grip. Drink now–1985.

1951

One of the poorest vintages since the early 1930s.
Mouton '51: Green, stalky, raw, just drinkable.

1952

A good vintage, rather stern and unyielding in the Médoc.
Mouton '52: Deep, fine, flavoury with silky/leathery texture. Drink now–1995.

1953

A very attractive vintage, a personification of claret at its most charming and elegant best.
Mouton '53: Deep and brown colour; glorious Mouton aroma of blackcurrants, cinnamon, and stem ginger. Rich, fine and flavoury. Drink now–2000.

1954

A rarely seen vintage.
Mouton '54: Despite its age a fairly deep, very rich appearance; bouquet fragrant and complex, but showing its years; very flavoury but drying out. Drink up.

Old wine, old bottles

1955

A good but underappreciated vintage.
Mouton '55: Very deep, yet looked a quick developer when young. Now medium-full colour; high-toned Cabernet aroma settled down to a beautiful, calm, dignified Pauillac bouquet. Delicate, flavoury, nice balance, very attractive. Drink now–1990.

1956

One of the more dismal postwar vintages.
Mouton '56: Deep, for an "off" year; medicated Cabernet aroma; very flavoury, piquant.

1957

Uneven, aggressive vintage.
Mouton '57: Lively deep red colour; appealing, somewhat piquant Cabernet-Sauvignon aroma. Very flavoury, richness masking '57 acidity. Nice now, and will keep.

1958

A curiously attractive but frequently maligned vintage.
Mouton '58: Deep coloured; very attractive, chunky, rich Cabernet nose; exciting flavour. Drink now–1985.

1959

The vintage of the century, though it has its detractors.
Mouton '59: Enormously deep in colour; concentrated Cabernet-Sauvignon aroma, cedar and blackcurrant; fairly dry, full bodied, massive yet soft, velvety, packed with flavour. Drink now–2030.

1960

A curious, somewhat overlooked year as was 1958, but more deservedly.

Mouton '60: Very pronounced cedar and blackcurrant Mouton aroma; very flavoury, exciting but short. Drink now–1985.

1961

One of the four best vintages of the century; deep, rich, concentrated, long lasting.

Mouton '61: A stunning wine. Still very deep but beginning to show a little maturity; amazing richness and ripeness of grape, concentrated Cabernet-Sauvignon bouquet, flavour; magnificent, balanced, unready. Drink 1985–2020.

1962

A good vintage, overshadowed, not surprisingly, by the incomparable 1961.

Mouton '62: At first a bit green, skinny, austere, and peppery nosed. Now has gained and developed in every way: very deep coloured; outstanding blackcurrant/mulberry bouquet; dry but very flavoury. Drink now–1990.

1963

A poor vintage.

Mouton '63: Sweet, clean bouquet; flavoury, balanced.

1964

On the whole a very good vintage.

Mouton '64: Unimpressive. Lacking fruit on the nose; rather skinny, short, and tailed off. Drink up.

Mouton Rothschild: the cellars

1965

One of the worst postwar vintages.
Mouton '65: Lost what little colour it had, very brown; none of the usual fruity intensity of aroma; a dry, thin shadow of Mouton, but flavoury and drinkable. Drink up.

1966

An excellent vintage, stylish, elegant, well balanced.
Mouton '66: Plummy colour; magnificently pointed Cabernet-Sauvignon aroma; dry, stylish, but unready. It should be excellent. Drink 1986–2000 plus.

1967

Quite attractive when young, and one of the last really good-value vintages of claret for the trade.
Mouton '67: Best in the mid-1970s, its sweet chaptalized nose at its most developed. With a fluffy, high-toned Cabernet-Sauvignon bouquet and flavour. Fruity but faintly tart and bitter. Drink up.

1968

A poor vintage.
Mouton '68: Light and very brown coloured; sugared nose; dry, thin, flavoury but tart.

1969

After a moderately promising start, one of the most unsatisfactory vintages of the period; flavoury but overrapid development.
Mouton '69: Curious, milky, un-Moutonlike nose, though it developed quite well; distinctly dry and green. Long, peppery, acidic finish but pleasant aftertaste. Drink now.

1970

An outstanding vintage, with a combination of bumper crop and high quality.
Mouton '70: Fairly deep, still youthful looking; fine but undeveloped nose, still peppery, characteristic Cabernet-Sauvignon aroma tucked under; a fairly powerful dry wine, more lean and austere than its peers. Drink 1988–2010.

1971

A good vintage with some stylish, elegant wines.
Mouton '71: Not very deep, with a sweet fruit-bush Cabernet-Sauvignon aroma; a dry, well constituted, fruity and attractive wine. Drink now–2010.

1972

A mean, uneven vintage, remembered more for its overpricing.
Mouton '72: Plummy, indecisive colour; not the usual Mouton intensity of aroma; dry, lacking body, with raw dry end. Drink now.

1973

A fairly light, abundant vintage.
Mouton '73: Fairly deep; underdeveloped bouquet, hard but refined; good long flavour, tannin, and acidity. Drink 1985–1988.

1974

A superabundant vintage, of moderate, uneven quality.
Mouton '74: Somewhat indecisive colour; fruity nose which opened up nicely; dry, medium body, straightforward, a bit short and raw. Interesting to see how it develops.

1975

A timely vintage of undoubtedly high quality.
Mouton '75: Hard and unyielding nose at first, fragrant but alcoholic, yet develops magnificently in the glass; on the palate, a dry, very hard, concentrated fruity wine of unmistakably first-growth quality. Plenty of tannin and acidity. A long laster. Drink 1985–2020.

1976

A good vintage.
Mouton '76: Deep coloured; sweet, high-toned bouquet, touch of vanilla (oak); good fruit under. An overall nice wine with medium body, good Mouton flavour and well balanced. Drink 1986–2000.

1977

Mouton '77: Not as pale as expected, though already mature looking; an open, light-character nose; fairly light in weight and style, distinctly dry. Drink now.

1978

Mouton '78: Fairly deep, rich plummy colour; broad, very sweet and attractive nose; nice ripe flavour, fairly full bodied, broad, easy, most agreeable flavour. Despite tannin and acidity nice to drink now but will develop. Say 1984–1998.

1979

Mouton '79: Deep, crisp, fairly intense youthful purple colour; youthful aroma, good fruit; dryish, medium body, nice vinosity, weight, and style. Dry finish. 1985–1995.

1980

A dismal vintage to open the new decade.
Mouton '80: Medium colour, rather plummy; sweet, youthful nose; soft and flavoury. A most agreeable light style of Mouton for early consumption, not long keeping.

1981

A vintage of considerable charm.

1982

A vintage of classic proportions and enormous promise. Experienced vineyard owners and managers said, almost to a man—or woman—that they had never in their lifetime known such a vintage. Time will tell.

Baron Philippe in the Grand Chai *about 1980, savoring the new wine in a glass held by the* maître de chai, *Raoul Blondin*

123

Little Brother Grows Up: La Baronnie

La Baronnie is the present trademark of the company in Pauillac responsible for marketing and distribution of all Baron Philippe wines. Having begun life very humbly as the *Société Vinicole de Pauillac*, it was acquired at the same time as Château Mouton d'Armailhacq, in 1933. Until 1939 the company was concerned solely with the production of *Mouton Cadet*, a brand name dating from 1930 and still at the time relatively unknown.

During the Second World War, the company's premises were entirely destroyed by enemy action, and in 1945 everything had to be begun again from scratch. Instead of setting up in Bordeaux itself, like most of the other wine merchants, Baron Philippe chose to stay in Pauillac, a small town of 8000 inhabitants in the heart of the Médoc, on the edge of his own estates. He bought a fine eighteenth-century town house, and made it his headquarters.

Despite frequent additions made necessary by the increasing volume of business and the expansion of the operation as a whole — bottling plant, cellars, stock rooms, and administration —

Brands from La Baronnie: a family group

*At the heart of a complex
modern organization: the
original headquarters of
La Baronnie*

Baron Philippe working on a label

125

the old house is still there, a link with the past but also the ultramodern nerve center of the company.

As the company has grown in size it has traded under different names:
· 1949 *La Société Vinicole de Pauillac* became *La Société Vinicole du Baron Philippe de Rothschild*. The trademark: *La Bergerie* (the Sheepfold).
· 1959 A new company name: *Baron Philippe de Rothschild, S.A*, the trademark remaining *La Bergerie*.
· 1982 The company adopted its present trademark, *La Baronnie*, a name better suited to the prestige of the operation and the quality of the product. The company is still officially called "Baron Philippe de Rothschild, S.A."

Employing a highly skilled staff of about 206, *La Baronnie* markets wine of different kinds and origins:

· *Château wines*, from Baron Philippe's own estates:

Château Mouton Rothschild: Roughly 100,000 bottles a year sold by the company (i.e., 30 percent of the crop) the remaining 70 percent being sold by the trade in Bordeaux.

Château Mouton Baronne Philippe: The company sells the whole vintage, roughly 200,000 bottles a year.

Château Clerc-Milon: Roughly 80,000 bottles sold by the company (i.e., 80 percent of the crop) the remaining 20 percent being sold by the trade in Bordeaux.

The brand names:

The *Appellation Contrôlée* regional wines: Pauillac AC, Médoc AC, Saint-Emilion AC, Pomerol AC, Sauternes AC, Graves AC.

The brands specifically created for *La Baronnie*: *Le Bouquetin*, *Le Berger Baron*, *Le Baronat*, and others, selected with the same care as the estate wines.

The two star performers, now world-famous, *Mouton Cadet rouge* and *Mouton Cadet blanc*, both selected with scrupulous care.

LA BARONNIE TODAY

La Baronnie makes 80 percent of its profits from the export trade. Its wines are available in 113 countries, of which the best customers are the United States, Canada, Great Britain, West Germany, Belgium, Switzerland, Holland, and Scandinavia. The elegance and style of the wines, the design of the labels, dynamic management, all go to make it the largest exporter of *Appellation Contrôlée* Bordeaux wine.

In 1979, *La Baronnie* embarked on a joint venture with the Robert Mondavi Winery of the Napa Valley in California, creating a new company, R.M.R. Vineyards. This company will produce and market a new wine, combining for the first time California grapes and production methods with traditional European expertise.

Having always been essentially a family business, *La Baronnie* has balanced a respect for tradition with a pioneering spirit: hence the loyalty and energy of the men and women who work there, every one of them aware of the high standard expected of Mouton Rothschild.

Opposite, three labels showing the respect for tradition and acceptance of change characteristic of the Baronnie approach. Note the development of the theatrical drapery and the crest.

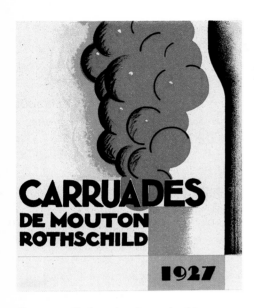

In 1927, all the wine from the Mouton Rothschild estate was sold under the name of Carruades de Mouton Rothschild

The first Mouton Cadet label, designed in 1933 for the 1931 vintage. It continued in use until the Second World War.

Above, the post-war label. Across the owner's initials, the old company name.

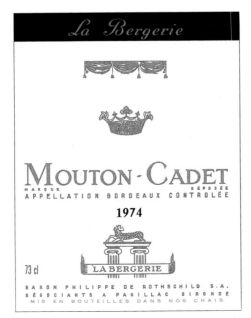

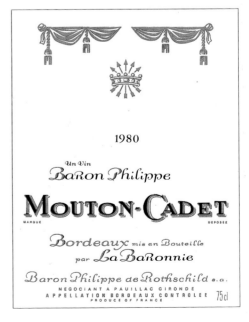

Talking of Wine

Années exceptionnelles
(Exceptional years.) Since 1900, the greatest years for red wine of the Bordeaux region have been 1900, 1920, 1921, 1926, 1928, 1929, 1945, 1947, 1949, 1953, 1955, 1959, 1961, 1966, 1970, 1975, 1978, 1981, 1982.

Appellation d'origine contrôlée
(AOC), or more simply (AC): The French regulations governing the amount of wine and geographical limits of the areas producing particular Bordeaux wines. The selection of these wines is based on precisely established local boundaries, the choice of vine, yield per hectare, and regular tasting by the authorities responsible. French law relating to wine production is the strictest in the world, giving *Appellation Contrôlée* wine a self-evident guarantee of quality.

Barrique
The barrel, traditionally made of French oak, and split along the grain of the wood to make an airtight joint. The barrel is used to collect the wine direct from the vat and to store it while it matures for two or three years before it is bottled. One barrel contains three hundred bottles.

Bouteille
In the Bordeaux region, several types of bottles are in use in addition to the classical Bordeaux bottle (*Bordelaise*) of 75 centiliters. These are the half-bottle (37.3 cl), the magnum (150 cl), the double magnum (300 cl), and the jeroboam (500 cl). The imperial (600 cl) was officially withdrawn in 1979 by international agreement.

Bouquet
Used loosely for the "nose" or general smell of a wine.

Cépage
The type of vine, depending on the region, best suited to the soil and the climate. In the Médoc, in the case of *Appellation Contrôlée* wines, the choice is further limited to cabernet-sauvignon, cabernet franc, merlot and petit verdots.

Chai
A local Bordeaux word for a storehouse where barrels are stored at ground level (as opposed to a cellar, or *cave*), used mainly for new wine. In high-quality château wine, the *chai* always faces north, to preserve an even temperature favorable to the settling of sediments in the wine.

In ascending order: the half bottle, the bottle, the magnum, the double magnum, the jeroboam, and the imperial

Château

A term used, principally in the Bordeaux region, to describe any wine-growing operation. The *Château* is taken to mean the estate as a whole: the vines, the vats, the storehouses, and the cellars. It may also include a house occupied by the owner.

Cru

A term in Bordeaux to mean a wine-growing estate of a certain importance or soil of particular excellence. The principal *crus* of the Médoc and Graves were classified in 1855 in five categories.

Cuve

A vat or a large container, holding up to 225 hectoliters of wine, in which the grape ferments. Traditionally the vats are made of French oak, split rather than sawed down the line of wood, in order to ensure airtight joints.

Egrappage

The separation of the grapes from the stalk.

Fermentation alcoolique

The fermentation: the sugar in the grape being turned into alcohol by the natural action of the yeast.

Marque

The brand name or trademark: the word or group of words that identify a product, in the case of wine the name by which it is recognized by the buyer.

Mout

(Must): The raw material from which the wine is made once the grapes are separated from the stalks; a foaming pulp of the skin, flesh, juice, and pips of the grape as it leaves the wine-press to slide down the chute into the vat. It remains in this state for about three weeks of fermentation.

129

Regions

The main regions providing *Appellation Contrôlée* Bordeaux wines are: Médoc, Graves, Barsac, Sauternes, Côtes de Castillon, Saint-Emilion, Pomerol, Côtes de Bourg, Côtes de Blaye.

Soins de la vigne

(Looking after the vine): The main work consists of plowing, pruning, and treatment.
· *Plowing:* Breaking up and aerating the soil.
· *Pruning:* This vital work is carried out according to a strict timetable, and involves the cutting back of last year's new shoots and preparing those that will carry the new grapes at harvest time. This is always carried out by specialists, as the quality of the wine, as well as the lifespan and future yield of the vine, depend on it.
· *Treatment:* Fighting the various pests and infections, such as mildew, that can attack the vine.

Tanin

Tannin, an essential preservative extracted from the skins of red grapes during fermentation. It dries the mouth.

Tonneau

(A tun): in present-day language, the same as a barrel. In specialized use among wine-growers, however, it refers to a measure of volume used in commercial transactions, and is the equivalent of four barrels, or 1200 bottles (900 liters), of wine.

Vinification

The action of transforming the ripe grape into must, and then, by alcoholic fermentation, into wine.

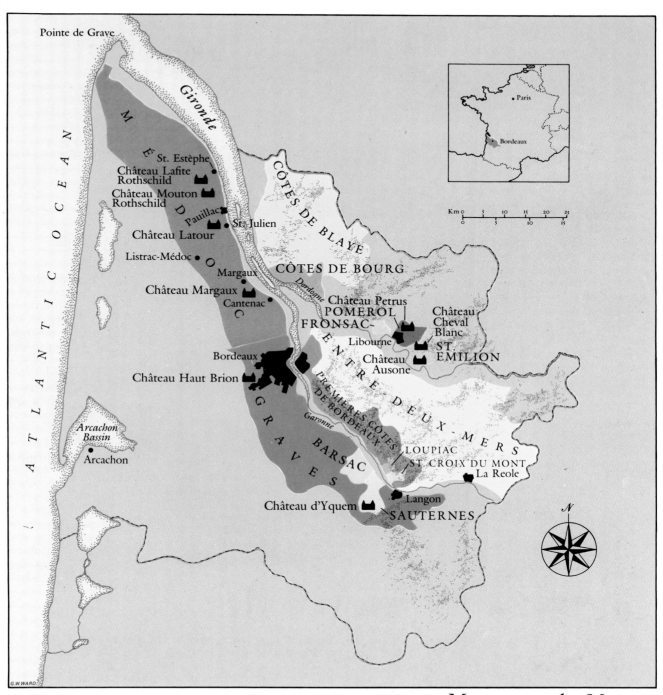

Pointe de Grave

ATLANTIC OCEAN

Gironde

MÉDOC

É St. Estèphe
Château Lafite
Rothschild
Château Mouton
Rothschild
Pauillac
St. Julien
Château Latour
Listrac-Médoc
Margaux
Château Margaux
Cantenac

Bordeaux

Château Haut Brion

GRAVES

Arcachon
Bassin
Arcachon

BARSAC

Garonne

Château d'Yquem

SAUTERNES

CÔTES DE BLAYE

CÔTES DE BOURG

Dordogne

Château Petrus
POMEROL
FRONSAC-
Libourne
Château
Ausone

Château
Cheval
Blanc
ST.
EMILION

ENTRE DEUX-MERS

PREMIÈRES CÔTES
DE BORDEAUX

LOUPIAC
ST. CROIX DU MONT
La Reole

Langon

Paris
Bordeaux

Km 0   5   10   15   20   25
0   5   10   15

N

Mouton on the Map

Visiting Mouton Rothschild
Visits to the *chais* and cellars take place every
weekday during working hours, except when
closed for holidays. Visits to the museum are by
prior arrangement only.

G.W.WARD

For Philippine

Wine

Born
It lives
But die it does not
In man it lives on

Heaven working
Nature moving in man
Soft as the soul moves
Seeking its source again

Mirror of those who have made it
A true grace, holding a sacred hope
The wine-god going among us in the glass
Bearing a message of age-old magic

May the work of great masters
Enliven each label
With echoes of Mouton
Fire and fervour

Year after year
This is creation
A work
Life

Wine

Papa (Baron Philippe)